STREAKING

Using Micro-goals to

TO

Achieve the Success You Seek

WIN

ANDRE JULIAN

This book is dedicated to:

My wife, who always has my back

My daughter, who inspires me to be my best

My mother, who never gives up on me

My father, who does his best

Streaking to Win

Using Micro-goals to Achieve the Success You Seek

Andre Julian

ISBN (Print Edition): 978-1-09834-560-0

ISBN (eBook Edition): 978-1-09834-561-7

CONTENTS

ACKNOWLEDGMENTS

Writing this book was a labor of love and the pages are filled with the voices, lessons and memories from my life. I'd like to thank God for His grace in my life, Christ for shedding His blood for us all and to acknowledge the people who ultimately made this book possible.

All my love goes out to my wife. Regardless of the situation, she always puts our family first and has a selfless quality to which I continue to aspire. I'm so grateful for our marriage and that she has made the choice to travel through this journey called life with me.

To my daughter, who has taught me the art of patience and who has truly been a blessing to me, even during her teenage years. She makes all my sacrifice feel like an easy Sunday morning.

To my mother, who had the courage to drag me to California and raise me on her own. I can't even imagine how difficult it is to be a single mom and I remain blessed to know her as both my mother and as my friend.

To my father, who may not have been naturally equipped to be a dad, but who really did the best he could with what he was given.

To Mark Munoz, who taught me that meekness is power restrained. You don't need to walk around like you have something to prove, you just need to have the ability to prove it when the time comes.

To my Godmother, Lianne Card. This book would never have been finished without her support, love, patience and hours of commitment to helping me find my voice.

To Jan Withrow and Rick Withrow, who both have made the choice to love me.

To my martial arts instructors: Alon Stivi, Mike Guymon, Michael Yawn and Jason Manly who all had the patience to teach me how to be a better version of myself each day. To Felipe Guedes, my current Jiu Jitsu instructor, who taught me that I am the Highlander.

To Michael & Carol Caito who have treated me and my family like a part of theirs, Job Tucker who has challenged me to reach towards new heights, George Moschopoulos who has been a true advocate and counselor, and Bill & Linda Smith who have served as the most amazing example of what a husband and wife, and parents, should be.

To Mickey & Wendy Gubman, Marc & Debbie Brener, Raffi & Stacy Adlan, Chris Bielecki, Jerry Bieser, The Brock Family, Anthony Caito, Scott Cohen, Anthony Costanzo, Don & Vena Currie, Micky Dhillon, Jake Ellenberger, Rob Gerstley and the entire Gerstley family, Chris Gray, Greg Halprin, Suheil Hazu and the entire Hazu Family, Texas Bob and the entire Holden Family, Steven & Karla Miranda, Pete & Amy Lou Mummert, Peter Navarro, Mark Pedemonte, Mike Peterson, Steve Petilli, Christian & Jina Provensen, Shawn Ray, Ovid Rijfkogel, Frank Ripullo, Steve Schroeder, Raja Shippen, Shalom Shalev, Sid Stankovits, The Taber Family, Anthony Vultaggio, Nancy Wallace and Robert Zamora who are the people in my life that have inspired me, mentored me, guided me, and have each given me the honor calling them a friend.

FOREWORD BY MARK MUNOZ

One Friday night at a church summer camp in Sebastopol California, which I looked forward to attending for the whole year, changed the course of my entire life.

The church camp staff was getting ready for what we thought was a message. Instead, the lights were turned off, a strobe light started flashing and the staff was yelling like it was a military invasion. As music was blaring with bells and whistles, we were blindfolded and subdued in a very playful way, each understanding that a game was soon to begin.

We were playing a seek and evade type of game called "Underground Church" and in order to win this game you would have to make it back to the sanctuary unscathed by "flour bombs" that were indiscriminately launched at you from all angles. A flour bomb was about 4-5 tablespoons of flour wrapped inside a Kleenex and secured by a rubber band. If you were hit by a flour bomb and the flour was on your clothes, you lost and had to go to the cafeteria because that's where all the losers went to enjoy refreshments. Well, I of course was going to win and was not interested in enjoying refreshments in the cafeteria.

We were in full camouflage gear as we knew that "Underground Church" was going to happen. We were blindfolded, guided to vehicles and then driven to certain spots of the campground. I was part of a group called "Mission Impossible." We were told that it was impossible for us to win because of the spot that we would be put in when we start the game. I, along with a group of five others, were loaded together in one vehicle. We drove up what seemed to be a steep incline with switchbacks for about ten minutes. The staff had placed us at the highest point of the campground where we had to scale down the side of a mountain to win the game.

After we were dropped off a whistle blew to signify the game had begun. As we took off our blindfolds, we instantly started hearing people screaming because they were getting pursued by the camp staff with flour bombs. The staff had flashlights that were flashing through the night sky as they surveyed the scene, while we had no flashlights and were literally being kept in the dark. It was completely chaotic and fun, and no one really knew where they were going, including me.

They often say that life is what happens to you while you're making other plans, and life definitely did happen to me during that evening at camp. Looking back, I'm not sure exactly what happened, because it all occurred so fast. As I was scaling down the mountain side, my vision became compromised because of all the shrubbery that began to envelop me as I pressed on ahead. As I was almost to the foot of the mountain, flashlights shone in the brush that I was in and the camp staff was awaiting my presence. Flour bombs began to be thrown in my direction. So, I decided to do what anyone who was going to win the game would do and scaled back up the mountain to get to a safer place. Flashlights were shining in the brush and I was running frantically through the woods and up this mountain. With almost no vision of the path before me, the last thing I remember, while still conscious, is falling into a ravine before everything went blank. Once I regained consciousness, there was one of the camp staff who had fallen on top of me and something was clearly wrong with my ankle. After shining a light on my ankle, I was horrified to see that it had been snapped in half, right near the ankle bone.

It was a while before help arrived. The camp staff was yelling for help. I must have gone into shock because my teeth were chattering, my bones felt cold and I could feel a throbbing in my ankle and foot. After pulling me up by a rope, there were about five camp staff around me. As they glanced at my foot and ankle, which was turned inwardly so much it looked deformed, I remember them saying, "we need to get him to the hospital!"

They called for help and about ten minutes later, which seemed to be about two hours, a car pulled up. I was placed in the back of the car. I remember going over bumps and thinking that my foot was going to detach and completely fall off my lower leg. The camp staff had driven me to a hospital and when I arrived, they had trouble accepting my insurance because my parents had military covered insurance. Long story short, I returned back to the campground after receiving no medical help, spent the night and left in the morning for home.

As I was in the back of the car, I was still dressed in full camouflage with little prickly sticky things poking me through my clothes and my ankle swollen so big that it had the same circumference as my knee.

When I finally got home, my mother immediately brought me to the Travis Air Force Base Hospital and, upon arrival, we were told that the hospital beds were all taken because of the Desert Storm War. So, my mother decided to drive fifty miles from where we were to the Oakland Naval Base Hospital. When we arrived, there was more bad news. They informed us that active duty gets full priority and that I would have to wait a week before I could be seen. As my mother was pleading with the nurse, there was a cancellation and I was admitted into surgery. It turns out that I had broken my talus, which is the weight bearing bone of your foot. It had actually been broken in half. Additionally, my calcaneus was dislodged from my foot and the tips of my tibia and fibula were fully fractured. Dr. Marlene DeMaio performed surgery, addressed my issues and drilled five screws into my ankle during the five-hour process.

My life wasn't at risk, but it might as well have been because I woke up to heartbreak. Although the doctors had diligently performed their task of fixing my ankle, there was only so much they could do. I was informed that I would never be able to play football again because of the severity and location of the break. I was devastated. Football was what I most loved to do, and a football player was all I wanted to be. Growing up in Vallejo, California, I was told that I had a promising football career ahead of me. In fact, many people were already telling me that I was destined for the pros, even though I was still only a freshman in high school. After all the years of work I had put into my football career, I had suddenly been sidelined.

Luckily, my dad had always taught me that we can't control everything in life so we should only focus on the things that we can control. Although football had meant so much to me, my consolation was that I might still be able to wrestle, which was a sport I had taken up in the football off-season. I never really had thought that wrestling was going to be my primary focus in athletics, but now it was all that I had. So, as with everything else I did in life, I gave it all my effort and wanted to be the best. It's pretty amazing how life works out for you, even during the darkest times. If it wasn't for that freak accident, who knows where my life would have led me. But, I'm grateful that it led me where it did.

After only a few years of wrestling I discovered that, for some unknown reason, it came very easily to me. Don't get me wrong, I worked extremely hard to get better and to catch up with those who had wrestled for years ahead of me. For people who have never wrestled, know that it is one of the most grueling sports on the planet. The college wrestling legend, Dan Gable, said the sport was so difficult that once you've wrestled, everything else in life is easy.

After only a couple of years of wrestling I won the California State Championship, then I won another. I also won two national high school wrestling championships and then went on to win the NCAA Division One national wrestling championship as a Senior at Oklahoma State University. When people ask me how I brought myself to overcome all the early adversity I had faced in my life, along with what should have been a career ending injury, to get to the level that I did, the answer was quite simple. I had faith that God had a plan for my life and that I was destined for greatness in whatever He chose for me. Simply put, I just knew that I was going to succeed.

After serving as an assistant coach at Oklahoma State for a couple of years, I moved my growing family to Davis, California to coach wrestling. So began another chapter in my life because I met Urijah Faber, who was one of the earlier faces of MMA. After coaching with him, he convinced me that I should come train with him in MMA (Mixed Martial Arts) and I fell in love with the sport. After only a few months of training, I won my first professional fight by knockout and was hooked. However, with four children and my budding MMA career, we needed help. After four professional fights, I moved down to Southern California because that is where my wife's family lived. I still remember the first day I walked into this little gym called Joker's Wild in a city called Lake Forest. It was recommended to me by a good friend of mine Michael Bruno who worked with Fairtex (a major brand in Muay Thai Kickboxing), as a place to check out and it was near my new house. Little did I know what an impact this little gym would have on my life.

I had trained at Joker's Wild a few times and it was already starting to feel comfortable to me. I showed up for a normal noon class and I wasn't paying too much attention to who was there because it always seemed like a good mix of guys. Then, I trained with a man who was a bit older than most of the rest, but he was really good. I was a bit surprised by how hard he tried and how he just didn't give up. As the weeks went on, he was a staple in the class and we started talking more and more about faith, God, training and all the other important aspects of life. As it turns out, I was talking to Andre Julian, who was one of the owners of the gym. Mixed Martial Arts and Jiu Jitsu were his hobby because his main business was in investments.

Looking back, it's kind of funny the way our relationship developed. He didn't realize that I was a professional fighter who was the NCAA Division One National Champion in wrestling and was one step away from a UFC contract. I didn't realize that he was the one financing the gym, ran his own investment firm and filled a lot of his days providing financial commentary on networks like CNBC, Fox Business and Bloomberg. The relationship started as a naturally developing friendship, which we still have to this day.

Fast forward a few years beyond our first encounter to when this little gym expanded into the Reign Training Center and Andre ended up as my business partner. We ran the gym throughout my UFC career and built a lot of lasting relationships while we were both blessed enough to be a part of it. One thing that continuously struck me about Andre is that he had this undying spirit of never giving up. He would train alongside professional mixed martial arts fighters that were ten to fifteen years younger than he was and hold his own. He would even join in on the conditioning sessions, which were three to five rounds of cardio brutally designed to prepare fighters to be in top condition for their fight. We would get our heart rates up to nearly 200 beats per minute for five minutes at a time, rest for a minute and then start again. Andre made it through the workouts without a problem. It was impressive.

When we talked about this elusive quality, that we like to refer to as "the fighting spirit," we came to the conclusion that it's something that can't be taught. People either have it, or they don't. People were either born with it or somehow developed it because of their life's experiences. Regardless of how people get it, it's a rare quality to have. As we shared some of the challenges that we both had faced in our lives, it became more apparent that getting through those challenges is what built us into who we had become as individuals. The question remained, when most people would have been broken in the face of our challenges, why weren't we? What was it that allowed us to move forward, conquer them, and become stronger in the process?

I recall an interview I once did right before a critical fight in the UFC. The interviewer asked me why I was so confident that I was going to win and I responded, "I just know it in my knower." It was my simple way of explaining that I don't know where this confidence comes from, I just know that I have it. I never could put a finger on that quality and how you achieve it until I read Andre's book.

Andre outlines a clear path to achieving this elusive quality called "grit" in a way that I've never heard and in a way that can actually teach you how to become successful in whatever field you set your mind to. Hopefully, the lessons contained in this book resonate with you and impact the way you live your life. I know that they've impacted mine. To this day, I still run wrestling camps and training programs and never thought that grit was something I could develop in my athletes that I coach. It seemed as if my job was to be a teacher and an inspiration to my athletes, in the hopes that they would operate at their highest level and champions would emerge. After reading this book and understanding the concept that Andre teaches, I now realize that I can truly influence my students by teaching them how to develop grit. I can't wait to see how many more champions I can build. My hope for you is that you take these lessons and build yourself up to be a champion in whatever it is you do, strive every day to be a better version of yourself, and embrace the struggle to see the results thereafter.

Mark Munoz

UFC Veteran

INTRODUCTION

Studying the reading habits of luminary entrepreneurs, Michael Simmons found that most of them only read twenty to forty percent of the books they purchase and many don't read any entire book after they begin.[1] He concluded that this isn't necessarily bad because people who love books tend to purchase almost every one they find interesting and simply end up with too many to finish. Many of the smartest people in the world have collections of books they never actually read. Because of this statistic I want to give every reader who picks up this book the opportunity to get everything they need from the contents, even if the book isn't finished completely. If you only read chapters eight and nine, you will absorb the main points of the book and you will be armed with the most essential ammunition to implement my strategy of success. I've organized the book this way because I want to give you the best chance of getting through the important content so you can reach the goals you've set for your life.

If you are an over-achiever or simply find the book interesting, then please read every last page. Otherwise, focus on chapter eight to learn the technique that will help move you towards the success you deserve and on chapter nine to learn how to implement the technique. My goal isn't that you love every word. Some of the chapters may not even resonate with you. Instead, my goal is that you learn a new strategy that will catapult you to levels of success that you never thought possible. Everything else in the book is built around chapters eight and nine, has been written to support the information they contain and has been designed to give you a deeper understanding of how to follow through with what you are taught.

Now that you have an understanding of how this book is designed, please read it as you must. Regardless of whether you read the entire book, the few key chapters or the parts that you simply find interesting while you are skimming through it; my hope is that it impacts your life in the most positive way. If you want to learn about my backstory, about some of the trials and tribulations I have encountered, and the challenges I had to overcome to come to this point in my life then start at the beginning. If you want to read some examples regarding how to apply what you've been taught, then continue to the latter sections of the book. However you choose to read this book, get ready to learn how to systematically change your life. Get ready to learn how to set out on a journey to reach your goals. Get ready to learn how to create an unstoppable belief in yourself and in your ability to achieve.

"When you start out to build a wall, don't think about building a wall. Instead, think about laying the next brick and the wall will build itself." -Will Smith

CHAPTER 1

Stranger in a strange land

Imagine standing in the middle of a packed stadium full of screaming martial arts fans, in a country that's completely foreign to you. You're minutes away from fighting a world-class heavyweight full contact martial artist that you've never met, and that you know nothing about. In my final year of graduate school that's exactly where I found myself. I should've been back at home in California diligently working on my Master's Thesis. Instead, I was in a city near the central coast of Israel named Herzliya, where students come from all over the world to participate in an annual full-contact Israeli Martial Arts championship. As I looked around at the crowd, at my instructor and at the man I was about to fight, it suddenly hit me that I was about to face one of the biggest challenges of my life.

It's moments like these that not only define us, but also let us live out the current definition of ourselves. Are we as strong as we think we are? Have we studied enough? Have we prepared enough? Are we good enough? Are we ready? It's thoughts like these that can paralyze us when we are about to face our fears. As I continued to gaze out into the crowd to soak it all in, these thoughts came at me like the rapid-fire succession of fireworks shot off during the grand finally of a New Year's Eve fireworks show. They were like the endless torment of a bully who convinces you daily that you could never stand up to them, so you might as well hand over your lunch money before you get hurt. Such thoughts can overwhelm you unless you get a grip on yourself and let reason override the mounting feeling of fear when you are about to face the unknown. Especially when that representation of the unknown weighs 220 pounds, is staring at you and wants nothing more than to kick you in the head.

I started training in an Israeli full-contact combat art called Hisardut® soon after entering college. After only five years of practice, there I was, standing in front of a trained Israeli soldier about to fight him for a world championship. Although I'd spent years developing the habit of overriding negativity and doubt with positive self-talk, no matter what I did, the negative voice in my head was telling me that I wasn't good enough. The voice continued to grow until it had reached a deafening level. Growing up I was a poor and skinny little kid who watched all the classic martial arts films and pretended that I was the hero. Now it was time for me to embody that role. But I was struggling to escape the fear and it started to take over my very being.

As the reality of that moment set in, I accepted it, took a deep cleansing breath and waited for the referee's signal to start. My opponent and I bowed to each other as a sign of mutual respect, the referee asked us if we were both ready and the drop of his hand signaled that the fight was on. As suddenly as it had started to take me over, that raging voice of self-doubt was muted by a tiny whisper coming from inside my head telling me that I was exactly where I was supposed to be. This new voice began to grow into a scream as I rushed in to face my opponent and then, in the time it took to cover the space between us, my mind became completely void of all thought and I knew that I had crossed over into a state of complete focus. There was no future, there was no past and only the present mattered. There was no more crowd, there was no more sound and I had no idea what was going to happen next. But, I was at peace with everything and still remember that first moment to this day...

"You can't connect the dots looking forward, you can only connect them looking backwards. So, you have to trust that the dots will somehow connect in your future." - Steve Jobs

CHAPTER 2

Backstory

Before you find out how that story ends, it's important that you have the backstory because wherever you find yourself in life there has quite certainly been a chain of events that led you to that moment. These events rarely occur linearly, are often full of bumps and the destination at which you've arrived can often be quite surprising. You see, by all intents and purposes, I really shouldn't be where I am today. If someone would have told the twelve-year-old version of myself that I would eventually end up owning several companies, become a financial commentator on television, fly in helicopters from Greenwich to Wall St., study at UC Irvine and Yale, come to the brink of losing everything and then find a way to build it back; I would have told them that they've got the wrong kid from the wrong neighborhood. I was just a poor kid from Upstate New York that was being raised by a single mom who immigrated to the U.S. to chase the American dream and was having trouble catching it.

My earliest memories of childhood were not of a kid who dreamed of eventually fighting in martial arts competitions and achieving success as a businessman, because these things didn't happen to the kids from my neighborhood. Instead, they are of my father abandoning my mother and me when I was only three years old and leaving us to fend for ourselves. In those days, we called the city of Buffalo home. If you've never been to Buffalo, it's an old steel town that once had a vibrant economy until the manufacturing industry changed, the jobs dried up and the neighborhoods slowly started to slip into a state of decay. It was a tough place to grow up because of the poor neighborhood we lived in, the bad weather and lack of opportunity.

I don't even really remember my mom and dad being together as my parents. Every once in a while, I get flashes of it. But they might just be memories conjured up from some of the stories my mom used to tell me. The last childhood memory I have of my father and mother in the same room is when I was four years old and they were no longer together as a couple. The memory is of violence and remains vivid in my mind. My mom was clearly distraught and was crying near the base of the stairs of my grandparents' home. My grandfather and grandmother were standing between the base of the stairs and the front door and my mother and father were arguing. It was difficult for me to understand what was happening. My father seemed quite angry and my mother continued to cry. Suddenly, my father forcibly shoved my mom down so that her back was planted against the stairs. As he stood over her yelling, his anger growing worse, he began to choke her. I was completely paralyzed and didn't know what to do. My mother was panicking because of a lack of oxygen from being choked. I started screaming at my father to leave her alone. My grandmother did nothing, but my grandfather calmly walked over, placed his hand on my father's shoulder and told him that it was time to stop.

That moment created a bond between my grandfather and me that was never broken. He seemed like the most powerful man in the world to me. Although my grandfather was much smaller in stature than my father, size didn't matter. In that moment there was no yelling and no fighting, but he projected pure authority. His calm voice and the touch of his hand brought my father out of his rage and made him come to his senses. As I later got to know my grandfather over the years, I came to realize that he exemplified meekness, that is power restrained. I have no idea how many times my father had previously laid his hands on my mom, because she refuses to talk about it. In a way, I'm grateful that my family was shattered before she had to endure a life of pain.

At the time, my mother didn't have a lot of options. She was a full-time student and a single mom. Because my father wasn't offering any financial assistance, she decided to make a journey down to New Jersey to stay with her sister's family for a while until she could figure out her next move. My aunt and uncle had a huge house, at least based on a four-year old's memory. There was so much room to run around and play, and all us kids made the most of it. My cousins were three, eight and ten years old at the time, so there was a lot of chaos during those summer months. There was even more of a ruckus when the kids from the neighborhood joined the fun. I can't describe the house fully, but I remember vividly that the house had a screen door leading out to the backyard. This became one of the cornerstones of my life story.

I can still clearly describe the details of that door as if it was right in front of me. On the bottom half of the door was a glass panel and a screen on the top half. The latch on the door didn't work. My aunt constantly nagged my uncle to fix it, but he never did. His procrastination was great for us. We had nothing to impede our progress as we raced from the house to the yard. As we ran out of the back of the house, we would get the door open by pushing on the glass, run down a few steps and jump right into the freedom of the backyard. One day, while I was going through my normal routine of running from the house to the backyard, I pushed on the glass panel of the door to open it and it didn't unlatch. Apparently, my uncle finally decided to stop procrastinating and fixed the lock. However, he didn't bother to tell anyone. Instead of jumping to freedom, both of my arms went straight through the glass panel as the rest of the door remained closed.

Even though the incident was many decades ago, I distinctly remember the sharp pain shooting up my arm and looking down to find that the glass from the window had cut me vertically down the inside of my left wrist. As my eight-year-old cousin called the hospital because no one else was home, I started to go into shock. My sharp pain turned into numbness as I stared into the gaping bloody hole in my wrist. The emergency team told my cousin to place a towel around my wrist and to hold it above my head in order to stop the blood flow to the area as much as possible. But, because there needed to be pressure applied to the towel, my cousin had to see if there were any shards of glass that need to be removed. Sometimes emergencies bring out the best in people and can mature them quickly. At only eight years old, my cousin carefully pulled out a triangular piece of glass from the gash in my wrist and hoped there weren't any more pieces as she wrapped my wrist with a towel and made me hold it on top of my head.

My aunt must have been somewhere close by in the neighborhood because I remember her coming into the kitchen just after the towel had been fashioned. As soon as she saw the blood-soaked towel, my hand on my head and shattered glass in the frame of the door leading to her backyard, she panicked. My cousin explained what happened very quickly to calm my aunt before she started to hyperventilate. At about this time, the ambulance showed up to bring me to the hospital.

When I arrived, their care was immediate. As soon as we entered the hospital, we were taken to a room where a doctor was already prepared to examine me. He immediately injected me with a local anesthetic to numb the area, picked out any remaining pieces of glass, scrubbed the area and started his stitching.

By the time someone contacted my mom and she could make her way to the hospital, I was already all stitched up. The doctor kept telling my mom that I was lucky to be alive and she relayed the message to me through sobs of joy. She explained to me that the glass had cut me to within an eighth-of-an-inch from my vein and, because it was a vertical cut, it would have most likely killed me if it had actually cut through that vein. If you cut your wrists horizontally, then you can be saved because there is a high probability that your vein is not severed past the point of repair. However, if the cut is vertical then your vein would most likely be severed and would be beyond repair. So, if you ever get to the point in your life that you feel as if you should end it, I have two things to say to you. One, don't do it! Please, reach out and get help. Two, don't ever slice your wrists vertically because there is no turning back.

Although the news of how close I was to death was the most frightening thing I'd heard up to that point in my young life, being told that I was lucky to be alive stuck with me for many years and made me feel special. Even during the toughest times in your life if you survive a close call and feel that you have a reason to be alive, you tend to value your life in a different way. You then begin believing that you are meant to be here for a reason.

After our summer in New Jersey, it was time to go back to Buffalo. Because we couldn't go back to the rooms we had previously rented, my mom could only afford to move us into an apartment on, "the other side of the tracks." It was difficult to transition and adjust to my new neighborhood. My mom was struggling to find her way, keep a roof over our heads and keep me fed. During this time in my life my mom went back to school and received government aid so that I had my three square meals a day. It never really dawned on me at the time that the food stamps coming in the mail, used at the grocery store to pay for everything we ate, meant that we had it tough. My mother never let on that we were struggling and always sacrificed to make sure I was taken care of. All I knew for sure was that my mother loved me. That made it a bit easier for me to keep a positive attitude because I knew that my mother was always there for me, especially when my life began falling apart.

What I haven't explained yet is that both my parents were immigrants from Ukraine, so I am a first generation American. Because of their shared loyalty to our heritage, they thought it would be a great idea to teach me Ukrainian as my first language, figuring that I would pick up English along the way. So I didn't speak or understand English, a barrier to assimilation with other children. When I was growing up, they didn't have English as a Second Language (ESL) programs. Instead they had the, "you'd better figure out how to speak English quickly so that kids stop making fun of the way you talk" programs. Not only did I seem slow to other kids, based on the fact that they kept asking me if I was "retarded," it didn't help that my ears stuck out sideways because I was born without any folds in them (the term "retarded" is used, not to offend anyone because I know the terminology is incorrect and insensitive. However, when I was growing up, this is what the kids called me. I can't change that and am only describing my youth as accurately as possible).

Although my mother always told me that God loved me just the way I was, she was also a realist and knew that kids would bully me because of my ears. Since I technically had a deformity, my mom found a way to get insurance to pay for corrective surgery on my ears so that they would look normal. She was always there for me, always full of love and always tried her best to protect me. But, as a single mom from a foreign country, she could only do so much. Life as a single mother was difficult enough for her, but having to finish her studies at the university and also work to feed me made it all the more difficult. Eventually, after years of being uninterested, my father told my mother that he wanted to be in my life more. At first, I was filled with excitement. However, that soon turned to constant disappointment.

When you're a young boy who doesn't have a lot of confidence and is constantly picked on by kids at school, the thought of having your dad in your life somehow strengthens your resolve. Although, for me that resolve slowly waned over the next couple of years as I came to realize that he actually had very little interest spending time with me. He had arranged for our visits every other weekend, but seldom showed up. My mom would help me pack my suitcase for the weekend and I would be all ready to go. Then I would sit by the front window of our apartment waiting for him to come and pick me up. When I grew up there were no cell phones and no way to reach anyone that didn't want to be reached. With no way to get in contact with him, I just waited for hours-on-end while my mother urged me to give up and go out and play. But, I didn't want to miss him when he arrived, so I sequestered myself in our apartment until Sunday evening rolled around and I finally would give up hope that he was coming.

He had endless excuses for his absences from these weekend pick-ups, but my mother knew that they were all covers for his spending time with the love of his life, which was the casino. His addiction to gambling grew greater over the years and didn't lend itself to much time with me. Even on the days that he actually showed up, he was more than likely to leave me with my grandparents while he took off to gamble. At the time, it broke my heart. But, looking back I realize that it may have been one of the most important times in my life because it gave me the opportunity to grow close to my grandfather. To this day, he remains my biggest role model and one of the most amazing people I have ever met. He passed away when I was 21 years old and there isn't a day that goes by that I don't think of him. He taught me how to be humble, yet how to stay strong. He taught me about having faith in God because, as a Ukrainian Orthodox Priest, that is where he got his strength. But, maybe most importantly, he taught me that we are all called to be great in our own special way and that our main goal in life is to figure out what that is.

Even though we didn't get to spend as much time together as I would have liked, the weekends spent with my grandfather were invaluable and helped to mold me into who I am today, even down to my love of boxing. My grandfather loved the sport of boxing and his favorite boxer was Roberto Duran, a legendary champion boxer from Mexico. What he loved most about him was that he was small, but tough as nails. This quality actually describes my grandfather. I think that he secretly always wanted to be a fighter, but never had the opportunity to pursue it because he had a family to take care of. It's a bit ironic when I think about it now. My dad living his life as an irresponsible gambler is what drove me closer to my grandfather, which is something that can never be replaced.

Eventually, my father's ego drove him to demanding sole custody of me, and he got his mother to help him build the case. It was much less about wanting me and a lot more about taking me from my mother. Like his gambling, it seems as if his relationships were much more about his winning than about having any thought for the other person in the relationship. Not too surprisingly, his mother was much the same way. As the pressure from them mounted, it became too much for my mother and she ended up kidnapping me. Literally. She determined that it was the only way to save me and to save herself from the constant torment of my father and grandmother. One day when I came home from school my mom had everything packed up, we went to the Greyhound Bus station and both got on a bus. This is how we ended up in California.

Moving to California was a way for my mother and me to get a fresh start and begin our lives over again, truly on our own. Fresh starts sound so great, but just because you leave the past behind doesn't mean that the past leaves you. The bullying that had been plaguing me in my past continued and even grew more physical the older I became. Eventually, it even became demeaning. When I was about ten years old, the neighborhood kids asked if I wanted to join them for a game of piñata. Thinking that they actually wanted to play with me, I decided to join them. It didn't turn out to be too much fun for me, but they had a blast. They handcuffed me to a tree and took turns beating me with a stick. I was the piñata. To add insult to injury, they left me handcuffed to that tree until just before my mother came home. After nearly three hours of torture, I was released and ran home to my mom with tears streaming down my face. My mom was horrified, but the only witnesses were the children who did it to me, and not one of them would admit it. They all got off without any punishment and had no remorse.

Soon, getting beat up on the way home from school, harassed by the kids in the neighborhood and my general inability to develop any sort of self-esteem became too difficult for my mom to witness. With no male role model in my life, she thought it might be time for me to finally have one. It turns out that my father had been trying to contact her through my aunt in New Jersey for several years and she thought it might serve me to have him back in my life. As hard as it was for her to reach out to him and let him know where we were, it was even harder for her watching me struggle tirelessly among my peers to fit in.

After not seeing him for almost five years, my dad came out to California, got a job and said he wanted to try to be a "good father" to make up for all the lost years. At first, I thought that I was in heaven. He played football with me, took me to the movies, hung out with me on the weekends; it was everything I ever wanted. Until reality set in and he started going back to his old ways of gambling, not spending time with me and disappearing for days at a time. When he wasn't out wasting his life away at the local casino, he was busy mandating that I had to do calculus proofs for four hours a day, in addition to my other homework. When you are in sixth grade, doing math you really don't understand for four hours every single day is torture. Now, it's important for you to understand that I truly believe my dad did the best he could. He simply wasn't equipped to raise a child. However, his inadequacies as a father actually provided the catalyst that started me on my journey to build self-confidence and to eventually compete for a world martial arts championship.

"Only a man who knows what it is like to be defeated can reach down to the bottom of his soul and come up with the extra ounce of power it takes to win when the match is even." - Muhammad Ali

CHAPTER 3

The fight

L et's get back to the moment before my fight is about to begin in Israel. In that brief space of time between my wrestling with my own negative thoughts and the referee signaling that the fight was starting, the realization hit me that my life's experiences had ingrained a level of almost irrational confidence within me and I was at peace with who I was in that moment. In *The Book of Five Rings*, Miyamoto Musashi describes the fifth ring void, which is where there is nothing or any form.[2] It's a state in which we are so focused on what we are doing in the present moment that we aren't thinking of the future and we aren't thinking of the past. Our mind is clear and there are no clouds of confusion. We aren't thinking about our stresses or our plans for tomorrow. Instead, we are so focused on what we are doing that in that moment time almost stands still. Everything becomes perfectly clear and we enter a type of flow state. Many athletes refer to this as entering "the zone." If you play basketball, the rim seems like it's the size of the ocean and you can't miss. If you play baseball, the ball seems to be twice its normal size and you can actually see the rotation of the ball as it spins towards you in slow motion. If you play soccer, the net seems like it's 50 yards across and 50 yards high when you set up to kick a goal.

Standing there, in that calm before the storm that precedes the moment of war and the war itself, there was no thought. My mind became completely blank. The noise of the crowd didn't exist, the nervousness of the unknown was gone and the only feeling I had was of nervous excitement because in my mind I had already won the fight. It was at that moment that I knew I was ready. If you've never been in a fight with a skilled fighter, it's tough for you to understand what it's like. Basically, there is no pain, there is no fear and your adrenaline becomes a controlled elixir that carries you through the initial phase of the battle. However, your adrenaline only takes you so far. At some point the reality of the situation catches up with your pain receptors.

Early in the fight, my opponent blocked one of my kicks with his shinbone, which means that we went "bone-on-bone." His block opened up a slight gash in the middle of my shin. It felt as though someone had just hit me in the shin with a bat, but I knew that it affected him as well. As we continued, it was clear that he was getting worn down. His defense was outstanding, so I chose to continue to attack without giving him any room to breathe because I had confidence in my conditioning. My tactic was working until I made an error. We were fighting bare knuckle, which exposes the hands to injury if the placement of your punches isn't perfect. Towards the end of the first round I wanted to hit him in the gut with a sharp uppercut, he moved a bit and I aimed a bit too low. The result was that I punched him right in the pelvic bone, sending a shock through my arm. Instantaneously,

I knew there was something wrong. Regardless, I finished the round strong and ignored the injury.

Once the round was over, my mistake became quite evident. My right hand had already become swollen and it felt as if a bone was broken. I asked the referee if I could tape up my hand really quickly, as long as it was completed before the start of the next round. He told me that if I attempted to tape up my hand in between rounds that I would be disqualified. Besides, there were only thirty seconds left until the start of the next round, so I wouldn't have time. Then, he asked me if I wanted to continue or if I was forfeiting. Without hesitation, the only choice I had was to continue on with the fight and adapt to the broken hand. With my acknowledgment to continue, my resolve reached a new level.

Because I could no longer punch with my right hand, I used my palm instead. A palm strike is not as powerful as a punch, but if it's carefully placed then it's still very effective. So, even though it seemed like a handicap, it was workable. Eventually, an opportunity arose that opened up the fight for me. We found ourselves a neutral position that involved a clinch, which is when both opponents are controlling each other, typically in a mirror-like fashion. Each may have one hand cupping the back of the opponent's neck to control their posture, and the other hand grabbing around the back of the opponent's elbow to limit their ability to strike or grab. In this case, we were also grabbing each other's *Gi* sleeves. If you aren't familiar with a *Gi*, it's a lightweight, two-piece (usually) white garment worn by barefooted martial-arts participants, consisting of loose-fitting pants and a wraparound jacket with cloth belt.[3] I suddenly gained a tremendous advantage when I dragged my opponent's left arm across his body to take him down to the ground. He reacted by trying to counter my strategy, and somehow his arm became stuck in my *Gi*. This move allowed me to land many unanswered palms strikes to his ribs along with a few kicks before we disengaged. This exchange provided me with momentum and the fight continued to swing my way. However, as we were coming to the end of the final round, I made another crucial mistake. I became too comfortable.

As we were close to the end of the final round, my opponent may have also been thinking that he was the star in his own martial arts movie and I was playing the villain from *The Karate Kid*.[4] Out of nowhere, he jumped up in the air, spun quickly and planted a spinning back kick that landed flush in my solar plexus. The kick came so fast, was perfectly executed and caught me completely off guard. For those who have never felt a heel kick straight to their solar plexus, to say it hurts is an understatement. It feels as if you just got hit with the butt end of a baseball bat. When a blunt force hits the solar plexus, the autonomic system of your body begins to shut down and there is very little you can do about it. At the point of impact, your brain tells you to crumble up into a little ball on the ground to avoid further punishment. The only strike to the body that might be worse is a liver shot, which has the same effect. After absorbing my opponent's kick, time slowed almost to a halt.

I could feel my nervous system shutting down and it was fighting my will to continue. In that moment, the biggest battle I was fighting was with myself. The referee was intently watching me to see what his next decision was going to be. Out of the corner of my eye, I could see my instructor's eyes grow wide and his face express a level of concern that he had never expressed before. Everything seemed as if it was taking place in slow motion. I could see the look of smugness on my opponent's face as he clearly thought that his kick was going to end the fight. The kick he landed was executed so perfectly. He must have been practicing and using it for years to devastate previous opponents.

He saw me as just another opponent who was about to succumb to his skill. What he didn't see was the years of abuse from the hands of others that I had overcome. What he didn't see are the hours of training I had put in and the pain that I had already endured to build the mental strength I needed to persevere in the face of overwhelming obstacles. What he didn't see is the sheer will and determination of the human being standing in front of him that had been forged through countless walks through hell. We are made up of all the things that other people can't see, good or bad. When people misjudge what we are made of it often leads to our greatest victories.

While standing there facing my opponent, during what seemed like an eternity, there was a complete conversation taking place in my own head. In real time, the decision I made only took about a couple of seconds, at most. However, in my mind, it seemed like it took ten minutes. Whenever we are faced with a challenge in life, success is not guaranteed if we move forward, but failure is almost always guaranteed if we don't. This was a defining moment that became a critical part of who I still am today. There was a clear voice inside my head telling me, "You didn't train for this fight for the past five years, fly to Israel when you should be back in California finishing your Master's thesis, and sacrifice thousands of hours to just crumble up in a ball on the ground and lose like a coward...get yourself together and do the only thing you know how to do...move forward!"

My feet felt as if they were stuck in shoes of cement, and my chest felt as if it was about to explode. However, I made the conscious decision to move forward because I knew it was the only way. As I did so, my opponent's shoulders shrugged in defeat and you could see the boldness in his eyes drain. I took a deep breath, mustered all the strength I could, and kicked him repeatedly in his thigh with my shin just as the final horn sounded to end the fight. My opponent and I embraced in acceptance of what we both just experienced and with the respect that instantly develops after two fighters just went to war with each other. It was now in the hands of the judges and, regardless of the result, I knew that I could hold my head high because I didn't quit in the face of adversity and could honestly say that I left it all in the ring.

As we both stood facing the crowd and were waiting for the decision to be read, I couldn't help but feel nervous. Much like the feeling you get sitting at the peak before the first drop of a roller coaster after you've endured the slow and torturous climb to the top, my heart was racing and felt as if it was going to bust through my chest. I wanted this victory more than anything I had previously set my mind to accomplishing and all I could do was wait. Finally, a judge walked the decision over to the announcer and there was no drama or drawn out process that followed. Instead, the winning fighter was announced, my arm was raised in victory and I was escorted to the medal ceremony.

Standing at the top of the podium with my hand raised as the champion was validation of my victory in the greatest physical fight of my life to that point. It wasn't just the fight that I'd won, but it was also a victory in the war that I had been waging against myself for years. All my effort, pain and sacrifice had been justified and I realized what I was made of and who I had become. Moments like these in our lives define who we are and add another brick in our wall of strength. However, the moments leading up to these moments are the ones that are truly necessary because they become the cornerstones of our foundation.

"I went to a bookstore and asked the salesperson, "Where can I find the self-help section?" He said that if he told me, it would defeat the purpose." - Steven Wright

CHAPTER 4

The premise

My hope is that you're reading this book for the same reason that I wrote it, namely, to learn exactly what you need to become confident, successful and to truly believe in yourself...that is, to be the hero in your own story.

After reading hundreds of books and watching even more videos on self-belief, motivation and success, I'm not here just to write another book that rehashes the same advice you've most likely heard many times. Instead, I'm here to point out what I think is missing from self-help and motivation material so that you gain the ability to follow through with the motivational advice that resonates with you most and so that you can truly live your best life.

If you've been searching for your success among all these books and videos, you've probably found that almost every purveyor of motivational material falls into one of two basic categories. They are the ultra-successful actors, Navy SEALS, or entrepreneurs who are sharing their wisdom with you about how they achieved uncommon success, or they are motivators who make a living teaching you how to be motivated based on their own research and experience.

In the first case, the accomplishments of the ultra-successful often seem so far out of reach that they seem a bit unrealistic. There is too much of a disconnect between where most people are currently in their lives and the lives of the ultra-successful. It's interesting to be inspired by Silicon Valley billionaires, successful commercial real estate developers and internet marketing gurus. But most people have a nagging thought that they could never be that successful, so they lose focus on their own goals and aspirations. The average person might have a will to succeed and gets momentarily inspired by stories of incredible success. They typically seek motivation because they have struggled with self-doubt, lack of discipline or the lack of a successful role model in their lives. This will to succeed often isn't large enough to get people to where they wish to go. If you are not already unusually successful yourself, it's very difficult to take advice from a successful billionaire because there's just too large of a gap between their success and yours. If the person you look up to has accomplishments that seem too far out of reach, then you will most likely stop reaching.

In the second case, motivators and success coaches have typically achieved their success teaching success principles to others. It's quite a paradox. As Nasim Nicholas Taleb astutely expresses in his book *Skin in the Game*, people fail to realize that the chief thing you can learn from, say, a life coach or inspirational speaker is how to become a life coach or inspirational speaker.[5] As Taleb observed, motivators have made their career by motivating. They don't teach you how to actually become successful in your career because they don't actually arm you with the specific tools you need. Instead, they are gifted at sparking something within you that gets you to operate at a higher level. Great motivational jargon coming from someone who's never been in your shoes and whose only success is in the business of motivational speaking may lead to temporary motivation, but not to lasting change.

In fact, many of the motivators in this second category even talk about the endless failures they endured in the workplace and how they rose up, not to actually be successful in the workplace, but to motivate others to find the success they never could find themselves. If you examine it, some motivational speakers were never successful at anything except motivational speaking. I'm not downplaying their success at what they have accomplished in the motivational world and think many of them are phenomenal at what they do. But I do find it interesting that an entire section of the motivational industry has been built by people who failed at most everything else in life and now are teaching others how to be successful. There is an old saying that those who can do, and those who can't teach. In the motivational industry, their saying seems to be those that teach, prosper.

Although these two categories of individuals differ, in both cases, the motivators typically try to fill you with inspiration by describing the hardships they had to overcome to finally reach their goals, and they expect that you will somehow overcome all of your personal challenges and roadblocks by getting strength from their stories. Although their stories are often outstanding, and sometimes will even bring you to tears, none of them teach you what you most you need to know, and that is a method that will arm you with the ability to get through the tough times that goes beyond temporary motivation. Many of them teach you tricks and hacks, but they don't teach you how to reprogram your brain so that you actually have the ability to follow through on an action plan leading you to your personal success. Again, their stories are often quite engaging, but you can't change your life based on someone else's story. You can't equip yourself to be successful without going through the process that it takes to be successful. You can't go through the process unless you've programmed yourself to push through the process when times get rough.

In the sport of skiing, a ski slope with a black diamond rating is said to be a difficult slope in comparison to others around it.[6] Imagine if someone told you that the hardest thing about skiing down a double black diamond ski run is that you have to simply trust in your ability and believe in yourself, and you will instinctively make it down the hill. Then, completely motivated, you go to the top of the mountain, make sure that your skis are on tight, and take the plunge past the point of no return. In that situation, you'd have no choice but to ski the treacherous slope that's beneath you. If you are a skilled skier, you might stand a chance. But, imagine if it's your first-time skiing. What are the chances you'll make it down the hill uninjured? The answer is that your chances are slim to none. It's just as ridiculous to think that if you don't believe in yourself that all you have to do is close your eyes, click your heels twice and repeat over and over that you do believe in yourself. It's just not going to happen.

Most of the advice you are given in order to achieve success assumes that you have the ability to follow through with the advice. But most people don't have that ability, which is why they fall short. This advice often consists of things like having you make a list of objectives that you need to accomplish, then telling you that you should consistently work towards accomplishing them. Another common piece of advice is that you wake up early and read a book for one hour on the subject you want to be an expert in and within five years you will be one. One of the best pieces of advice is to make discipline an integral part of your life and exercise every day to strengthen the body-brain connection. These are all great words of wisdom, and I believe that each of them will obtain some positive results.

Most people fall short taking action on such advice because they are being told "what" to do, but not "how" to become the type of person that will actually follow through and do them. You literally have to be sequestered in a remote part of the globe to NOT know what to do to become successful. If you are one of the people who tries to follow all these prescriptions for success but continues to fall short, often blaming yourself, then stop beating yourself up! It's not your fault. If you've listened to all the motivational audio, read all the motivational text and watched all the motivational video and still aren't any closer to reaching your goals, then you need to make one change allowing you to follow through with all this great advice. You need to reprogram your brain to create a personality within yourself that will give you the ability to actually follow through on what you start.

This book will teach you exactly how to create this reprogrammed personality by following a very simple process. Please understand that most success is not found amongst the elite of the elites. Instead, it can be found among hard-working people who commit themselves to their craft or industry, apply themselves day after day and create a great life for themselves and their families. Such people have a specific quality that allows them to sacrifice themselves, and hours of their lives, to committing themselves to a vision. Most of them don't own a private jet, they don't own a Rolls Royce and they don't eat lobster and caviar every night. But, they have tremendous lives, live in great neighborhoods, drive desirable cars, send their kids to college, vacation wherever they want a couple of weeks out of each year and get to retire well. These people represent the typical success story, available to those who have the ability to shut out the noise, focus on the prize and work towards the vision they have set for themselves.

Unfortunately, almost everyone in our society searches for easy answers and even easier solutions. Some include trying to develop abs in six minutes without changing their diet, to believing they can hack their way to success by working only four hours a week. We are a "get rich quick, lose weight without eating properly or working out, still reaching the pinnacle of success by wishing it into existence" society. Those who find success understand that it never comes before hard work. Persisting at something you believe in, day after day, month after month and year after year is what will ultimately define who you are and what you become. As positive as that sounds, most people never become the best version of themselves and continuously fall short.

Thomas Edison once said, "A dream without action is just a hallucination." This book was written to help you understand how to envision the life you want and then learn how to follow through on the things you need to do in order to achieve the vision you created. After all, most of us know what we need to do, but we don't do it. Most of us know how we need to eat to be healthy, yet eat unhealthy food. Most of us know that we need to have a consistent workout regimen, yet don't follow one. This entire book is focused on providing the specific tools you need that will program you to take action consistently. It's not just about the "what" and the "how." It's also about separating yourself from the masses who dream, and instead becoming part of the special group who actually live their dreams.

Please don't get me wrong. I love the great motivators who inspire us. I love Les Brown, Anthony Robbins, Inky Johnson, David Goggins, Jocko Willink. The list goes on and on. These speakers and authors have a tremendous insight and wisdom to share. The problem is that so many people listen to these great motivators, yet few people can implement any of their teachings. I wrote this book to share a method that will actually create that ability within you and to follow through with what you start and apply all the great motivational advice that you love. The goal of this book is to supplement the information you already know from all the great motivators you follow, get you off the sideline of your own life and become the hero of your own story by learning a method that will finally allow you to follow through on working towards the objectives you have set for yourself. If that's what you are after, then let's start by understanding the power of belief, how to prepare yourself to create it and then how to apply it to reach your goals, dreams and aspirations.

"Believe in yourself! Have faith in your abilities! Without a humble but reasonable confidence in your own powers you cannot be successful or happy." – Norman Vincent Peale

CHAPTER 5

Why do we fall short in our quest for success?

Starting is one of the most difficult things for people to do, that is why most people don't live up to even a fraction of their potential. It's why ideas are left in the memory banks of the well-intentioned entrepreneur, while they end up being brought to life by someone else who was simply able to execute. It's why so many people hesitate when they are faced with a decision and often miss out on the great opportunities that slip away. It's why most people are observers and not participants in their own life, a condition that ultimately leads to a life not lived.

If you are one of these people, then you are not alone. In fact, no one is completely immune from the diseases of laziness, procrastination and doubt. If this is the case, then what is the secret sauce to success? The answer is simple. To be what you want to be you need to do what you need to do. That's it. Everything that we accomplish in life is based on our actions. Describing these actions is at the core of most motivational literature and the gap that most people face is being able to follow through. We all know that discipline, consistency and resilience in the face of adversity are qualities we should demonstrate. So, the issue is not with the motivational programs because, as we've already touched upon, most of the advice is sound. The issue is that it's nearly impossible to follow the advice that is being prescribed because it's very tough to follow through with a program that requires intense discipline unless you already have that discipline. It's also difficult to power through obstacles you may encounter relying on someone else's strength.

There is an old saying credited to an anonymous author that an intelligent person learns from their own mistakes, but a genius learns from the mistakes of others. That's a great quote and quite eye opening. If you want to understand why so few people learn from other's experiences, it's because so few people are geniuses. Mensa, the international intelligence organization that only extends membership to people they deem as geniuses, defines a genius as someone who has an IQ in the top two percent of the population. Some people in the organization even think that this criterion is a bit too lax, but it's a very commonly accepted global definition. If we accept this definition, and only geniuses can learn from other people's experiences, then only two percent of the population can learn from the experiences of others. But, with this limitation, how do the other ninety-eight percent achieve success?

The idea came to me some time after I had the opportunity to speak at a TEDx event in 2016 on the topic of learning how to believe in yourself so that you can overcome any challenge in life as you forge towards success. The premise of the talk was that motivational speakers focus on all the things you need to do to become great, *after* you have achieved the first step of believing in yourself, while ignoring that believing in yourself is the hardest step. After sharing my philosophy that learning how to believe in yourself comes from overcoming challenges that rewire your brain to create that belief, in true TEDx fashion, I asked something of the audience: "I don't know where you are in life, or what mountains you have left to climb. But, I would ask that you find your own impossible task to conquer, find your own story to tell and create an amazing belief in yourself. Then, whenever you can, please help someone else do the same."

What a great "TEDx" action item! I was impressed with myself and really thought my talk would be effective in helping people. However, although my goal of teaching people "how" to believe in themselves was completed during the talk, my goal of giving the audience the "ability" to reach that goal was not. I had missed the mark. At the beginning of my talk, I focused on my belief that motivational speakers attempt to motivate you with their own stories to teach you how to reach success in you own life, yet I offered no real solution that was any different. Having failed in my mission, I became obsessed with figuring out how to correct it. Then, one day, inspiration hit me. There was a commercial for the AMP© energy drink that showed a Mixed Martial Arts fighter waiting for the bell to ring right before a fight. The camera dramatically zoomed in on his stone-cold face and the tag line was, "Before every moment, there is a moment." Instantly, I understood what I needed to do.

Realizing that my fifteen-minute talk had fallen short of my goal of truly teaching people how to fill the gap between where they are and where they want to end up, it was time for some analysis to figure out what was missing. Although my goal was to elevate the content of my presentation beyond typical motivational speech, I had jumped right into the same pool with every other speaker who shares their triumphs of overcoming obstacles they had faced in their own life, and then fails to effectively influence any real change in anyone else's. Although sharing personal stories is important because it connects the audience with the speaker and builds credibility, the impact should come not from the story but by affecting real change. This book was written for the sole purpose of impacting those who read it, first through sharing my journey and the lessons I learned along the way, then by explaining exactly how to implement a very specific method that will teach people the steps they need to take to believe in themselves and to reach the success they seek. My hope is that the content within these pages impacts your life and is a catalyst for positive change.

To create the life you envision, you must not only understand the formula to success, but also need to learn how to follow through on what you need to do. Ideas and a vision are simply not enough. You need to own the tools that drive you to take action in a consistent fashion to execute your vision. It's not about the "what," but it's about separating yourself from the masses who dream about "what" and become a part the small group of the elite who actually create their dream. But, how do you do that? Les Brown, who I think is a tremendous motivational speaker, once said that the easiest thing he ever did was make a million dollars in one year. But, the hardest thing he ever did was to believe that he could do it. If the hardest thing you will ever do on the path to success is to believe in yourself, then let's focus to teach you how to believe in yourself so that self-doubt and negative self-talk don't exist in your thought process. Almost all motivational material focuses on everything you do after you already believe in yourself, and this is why it falls short. Let's tackle accomplishing the hardest thing you will ever do, first. Then, we can tackle the rest.

*"It's not how good you are, it's how good
you want to be." - Paul Arden*

CHAPTER 6

Creating belief in yourself

In today's society we're inundated with motivational programs
promising abundance and success based upon very straightfor-
ward advice that seems like it would be quite easy to follow. Little
motivational quips, like the following, are supposed to inspire us
enough to get us past all our adversity and eventually create the life
we dream of:

- Write down your goals every day and visualize that you've
  already achieved them.
- Act as if you already have what you want, and success will
  come to you.
- Use positive self-talk to counteract negative thinking.
- Don't focus on the goal but focus on each step along the way.
- Don't hesitate in your decisions to take action.
- Wake up an hour earlier every day and exercise to set the tone
  for the day.
- Know your "why" and you can overcome any "how."

These, and many other pieces of advice, aren't secrets that only the privileged few know. In fact, writing down goals and visualizing your success in achieving those goals has been rewritten, repackaged and represented again and again with each "new" motivational program that's released. One simply has to search for the words "success" or "motivation" on the Internet and these secrets to success and fulfillment pop up in droves of inspirational blogs, vlogs and videos. But, even though we have easy access to these formulas of success, why is it that so few of us are able to apply them for a sustained period of time while in pursuit of our goals, dreams or aspirations? If you listen to the experts on the subject, they say that if you aren't succeeding in your quest for success it's because you don't believe in yourself. Then, they go on to tell you that all you have to do is first believe in yourself, and then everything else will come together for you. That's right, just let go of all your insecurity and self-doubt, snap your fingers and believe.

That's great advice! However, what if you don't know how to believe in yourself? You might know the "why" that motivates you and the "what" that you're seeking. However, if you aren't born with the "self-belief gene," or haven't been conditioned over time to develop it, then all the advice in the world telling you to believe in yourself won't help because there's something missing; there's a gap between your current self-image and the self-image you need to have in order to be successful.

To truly believe in yourself you must find a way to fill this gap.

Very often, our past can provide us with clues that will help us create our future. To fill my own gap, it was easier than it might be for most because I had a significant emotional event when I was quite young that actually helped to rewire me for success. To help put you in the frame of mind that will best allow you to understand what I went through, think back to some point in your life that you had a burning desire to achieve, acquire or accomplish something important, but faced tremendous challenges. What was that toy, outfit, dream job, mission to give back, or simply that, "just wait until I'm an adult" dream that you had when you were 10, 12, 15...maybe even now? It has to be something that's so motivating that you can't stop thinking about it and would do anything to get it. Once you have that goal firmly set in your mind, you'll be in the same state that I was in as a twelve-year old who was on a quest to reach the biggest goal of his life.

When I was twelve, my one great desire was to own a chrome-plated Diamond Back BMX bike, with Oakley grips, Dia-Compe Alloy Brake Levers, and a laid-back GT BMX seat post. Now, compared to some of the dreams each of you might have envisioned, I understand that portraying my BMX bike as the ultimate object of my desire may seem a bit anti-climactic or even a bit too small of a dream. But, there was a serious "why" attached to my desire. In my neighborhood if you didn't have a BMX bike, you were an outsider and you weren't accepted. Before heading back to Buffalo for a second stint, I was living in Southern California at a time when all the cool kids would meet every Saturday and Sunday morning at a make-shift BMX racetrack that was built behind the Middle School we all attended. This place was where you tested yourself against the other kids and established the pecking order for the next week. True legends were built during those weekends and if you weren't a part of the scene, then it was social suicide. So, my desire for the bike was much more about my need to somehow "fit-in" than about the actual bike itself.

There were three major obstacles keeping that bike out of my reach: I had no money, no job, and my potential loan officer (my dad) thought that BMX was a ridiculous hobby and a complete waste of time. That evaluation is quite ironic because his favorite hobbies were cocaine, blackjack, and abandoning me for days at a time to do cocaine and play blackjack. But, that's a story for another time.

So, my only hope to obtain that bike was to earn the money somehow. I applied to a music store to stock shelves, a restaurant to wash dishes and local ballpark to sell popcorn. Each time being told that child labor laws prohibited me from working until the age of six-teen. So, I scoured the neighborhood for odd jobs and had no luck with my search. Desperate, I did what any resourceful twelve-year-old did to earn money in my neighborhood...I sold drugs. Of course, I didn't sell drugs. Yet, the thought did cross my mind. After all, I might have had my first customer in my very own home.

With my options exhausted, I resorted to an inherent skill that twelve-year olds call upon when they want something they can't have and their parents continue to say no. Anyone who has a teenager is very familiar with it and it can get quite unnerving. I resorted to nagging and incessantly begged my dad to buy me that bike.

"Please, Dad! I'll never ask for anything again, ever! I'll wash the dishes every night, clean my room every day and do extra chores. You'll never hear a complaint out of me. I'll be quiet as a church mouse and I'll even wash and wax your car every weekend." It's amusing what we will commit to doing if the reward is great enough. None of my begging worked, at first. But, somewhere along the way I had a breakthrough and uttered a key phrase that resonated with my dad like the number 21, "I'll do anything to get that bike!" With that one simple statement, my dad smelled a wager.

We had a pair of seven-and-one-half pound cheap plastic dumb-bells that happened to be lying in the room when I made that state-ment. I'd started using them to work out with because I was attempting to "bulk-up" in order to stop some of the bullying that had plagued me continuously. I was a skinny little kid that made an easy target. I thought that becoming muscular would stop the kids from picking on me. To give you some perspective, after many months of training, I could do about ten repetitions of bicep curls with those weights. On a good day, I might have been able to struggle to fifteen repetitions, a very unimpressive number. During our discussion, my dad noticed these plastic dumbbells lying on the floor and conjured a bet. The bet was simple. He told me that if I could do 500 curls in a row (yes, 500 in a row) that he would buy me that BMX bike. But, if I couldn't, then all bets were off and he would never hear of my desire for the bike again.

As usual, Dad's goal was NOT to help me get the bike, but to set me up to fail. He wanted to make a bet that was so outlandish that there was no way he would have to buy me that bike. In fact, this 500-curl challenge was so outside the realm of possibility that he could've just as easily handed me a lump of lead, a book on Alchemy, and told me that I could sell the Gold that I manifested from the lead to pay for the bike.[7] With Dad, I always felt as if I was the subject of some strange psychological experiment and that everything he did was some kind of test. It was as if he was taking notes on my reactions to later write about in some scientific journal. Regardless, my mind was fixated on that BMX bike and I took the bet.

With the smell of Dad's stale cigars and red wine filling my nostrils, there I was, standing in front of him with a pair of dumbbells in my hand; facing this impossible challenge of 500 curls. Just as I was ready to start, my dad pinned my shoulder blades against the wall so that I couldn't cheat. If I was to win this bet, then I would need to use perfect form and wasn't allowed to swing my arms to gain momentum.

One-by-one I curled those weights, as if the impossible accomplishment of completing 500 curls by a skinny twelve-year-old kid might actually occur. When I first started, I have to admit that I wasn't sure if I would make it to even twenty repetitions, even though I wanted that bike so badly. But, I figured that I had nothing to lose because before I started the bet, I didn't have a BMX bike. So, even if I failed, I wouldn't be in a worse position than before I had started. In fact, my position wouldn't have changed at all, so there was nothing for me to lose and everything to gain. However, the further I continued to push myself, the more focused I became on actually getting to those 500 reps.

100 reps in…my biceps went beyond discomfort and really started to ache.

200 reps in…I was covered in sweat, but this was about the point at which I started to believe that I might actually be able to pull it off.

300 reps in…my grip started to weaken, and I suddenly started to doubt. This felt like when you don't want to make two trips from the car to the kitchen and mistakenly think you can take in ALL the bags of groceries in one trip. You know the feeling; your biceps are burning and your hands start to go numb as the weight of carrying too many bags starts to cut into the circulation of your fingers.

400 reps in…my whole body began shaking and my biceps felt as if they were slowly detaching from my tendons. It was as if someone was taking razor blades and slowly chipping away at the base of my bicep tendon. With every rep feeling like my biceps were about to be sliced off and separated from the bone, I started to imagine myself with torn biceps, with no bike, and laying curled up in a ball in the corner feeling sorry for myself.

Then, something strange began to happen. About as I crossed the 450-rep mark, the background noise of the TV slowly grew mute, the smell of cigars and wine dissipated, and the torturous pain of muscles strained beyond their capacity was strangely replaced by a comfortable numbness. Looking back, I realize that this was my first experience of being in the "zone." There was no past, there was no future and the present was all that mattered. Each curl became just another number and my only focus became to do just one repetition, which was the next repetition. The end goal of getting the bike became irrelevant and the realization that it would eventually come if I could just muster up enough strength to do that next repetition is what drove me to forge ahead.

Then, at a point nearing 500, my hands became so wet from sweat that I could no longer hold the weights. But, Dad was kind enough to put wads of toilet paper in my palms to soak up the sweat. At this point, I believe that something must have shifted in Dad. At the start of the bet, I think he just assumed I would quit soon into my effort and he would be off the hook for ever having to buy me that bike. But, after witnessing my torturous commitment to my mission, giving me this assistance might have been his way of letting me know that he might actually be a little bit in my corner.

After about forty minutes of bicep curls, I remember suddenly stalling at 498, then barely getting to 499 and feeling as if, all of a sudden, the weight of all my previous failures was keeping me from that last repetition. These thoughts, however, faded. Oddly enough, they weren't replaced by the vision of that BMX bike, or of the impending acceptance by my peers, or even with the prospect of finally winning a bet with my dad. Instead, they were replaced by the pride I'd just developed in myself that I'd never felt to that point in my life. I, a skinny little kid, was about to accomplish the impossible against every law of physics, because somehow my will to succeed was greater than the impossible challenge before me.

Suddenly, the vision of the BMX bike was replaced by strength, confidence and a sudden burst of self-esteem. Like some kind of tribal right of passage, I'd walked through the fire and now had transformed myself into someone who believes, not only in a vision, but in themselves. One repetition from my goal the weights in my hand became feather-like and my mouth suddenly began to water with the taste of accomplishment. At that moment, something in me made me believe that I could do one million reps if I had to. In fact that 500th rep was easier than the first.

Conquering this challenge changed my life. Before this experience, I didn't believe in myself at all. I'd wished there was a magic self-esteem pill I could take that would somehow transform me into a winner, and there wasn't. It wasn't until I conquered my own impossible task that I transformed my belief from self-doubt into self-confidence. At the time, I really couldn't comprehend what had just happened on a psychological level. But, I knew what the feeling of greatness was like for the first time in my life.

"When writing the story of your life, don't let anyone else hold the pen." - Harley Davidson

CHAPTER 7

How to create success

It wasn't until years later that I would come to understand just why my 500-curl experience had so profoundly defined my self-belief. As I got deeper into my courses in Cognitive Psychology at the University, I started to learn that there were some very real physiological changes that I had experienced when I was that skinny little kid doing those 500 curls. Studies of the brain, like the ones done by Nobel Prize winning Dr. Susumu Tonegawa at the MIT School of Neurobiology, help to explain how the process I went through actually changed my self-belief in a very real way. Tonegawa found that when we experience an event, it programs a specific sequence of neurons firing in our brain, which become linked to that experience.[8] Whether it's learning to believe in ourselves or learning a simple math equation like $1+1=2$, there's an experiential element within the learning process. Therefore, when we're going through an experience, an original frame of reference is created that leads to the construction of these specific neural pathways and gives us the ability to reconstruct those pathways when we face a similar task or circumstance in the future.

You can teach a child the 1+1=2 formula for years and they'll stare at you blankly each time you go over it, until that one pivotal moment where the light goes on and they get it. This "getting it" experience results from the programming of the brain finally being recalled and then firing in the correct sequence. Although Tonegawa's studies explained that my belief was transformed because of my experience, they didn't explain why this change had occurred so quickly and based upon only one event. However, the speed of my transformation was explained in a study done by Nobel Prize winning behavioral economist, Daniel Kahneman. He found that when we have an experience, whether it's good or if it's bad; the more intense the experience, the more we remember it and the deeper it gets ingrained into our psyche.[9] So, experiences not only help to program our neural networks, but also help to define their strength based upon the strength of the experience. Therefore, if we are lucky enough to have an intense experience that allows our neural networks of confidence to develop quickly, then we can develop lasting change in a short period of time.

For this same reason we can instantly build all kinds of neural networks through our various experiences. Simon Sinek, the motivational speaker and author, discusses this phenomenon when he describes building instant relationships of trust in his book *Start With Why*.[10] He gives an example of an instant connection of trust that can be built and how our brains are already programmed to build this connection. Imagine if you are in need of a babysitter and you really need to find someone you can trust to watch your child if you are going out for the evening. This decision is not really about the experience or resumé of the babysitter. Instead, it's about finding that person who you trust will take care of the most valuable entity on the planet to you, your child, while you are out for the evening.

Sinek describes two options for finding a babysitter in this scenario. The first choice for the job is a sixteen-year old just down the street, who lives in your community but may not even have any baby-sitting experience. The second choice is a thirty-two-year-old who just moved into the community from an unknown place but has ten years of baby-sitting experience. The question becomes, whom do we choose? Most people would entrust their child's care to the sixteen-year-old because, even though they are young and have no experience, they come from within the community. You don't even need to know them personally, but instant trust is in place. Because you are both from the same neighborhood your brain forms a quick judgement that you also share in the same values and beliefs, which allows you to make a more immediate connection. In this scenario, the brain had already built a set of neural pathways that linked the shared experience of community to a strong level of inherent trust.

If experiences are the "secret sauce" to our learning process and are a key to building neural networks, why then do we skip over this secret sauce when it comes to believing in ourselves or when it comes to building confidence? A child can't expect to learn the concept of math the first time it's introduced, nor can we expect to believe in ourselves until we've actually experienced belief in ourselves first. This is seemingly a paradox because our brains need to be able to recall and recreate a sequence of neurons firing in a pattern of "self-confidence" when we need confidence to face a new challenge. Therefore, we had to have faced and overcome similar challenges in the past to create this sequence. The only obstacle separating you from whom you ultimately want to be is an experience that bridges the gap of self-belief you currently hold. Why not put yourself in the position to go through the experiences necessary to fill that gap? If you don't, no matter how big your "why" is, your "what" may never come.

In the previous chapter, I could have shared other stories in my life of overcoming years of abuse, my brushes with death early in life, and of how I turned my biggest failures into success. Why didn't I share some of these other stories? Instead, why did I choose to tell you a story about kid, a bike and a set of dumbbells? Remember, my goal isn't to motivate or inspire you based on my story. My premise is that you can't actually get motivated based on my experiences. The process that we go through in order to rewire our brains is so much more important than the story itself. Most motivational material typically focuses on motivation through inspiration, but not on the process people need to go through in order to actually create their own motivation. Such material focuses on others overcoming their own personal tragedies by putting the audience into an emotional state of empathy. But empathy doesn't have a lasting impact. I am much more interested in the process than the feeling of motivation because it is the process that leads to change, while the feeling subsides.

I also shared a personal story that you might not even relate to, specifically because it's my story and started me on my path. The experience had a personal impact on me, but wasn't really meant to impact you in a way that would inspire you to reach all your goals. That would be empty motivation. You might be motivated for the moment, but that motivation wouldn't outlast the reading of my story. Once you put the book down to go out and face your own challenges, you will most likely forget about my silly BMX bike, my 500 curls and my emotional battles with my father.

My goal is for those who don't have their own story to go out and find one, instead of hoping that someone else's will work for them. What's missing from the current psychology of motivation is the acknowledgement that we can't believe in ourselves based on someone else's story and need to find our own sense of belief. Only by overcoming our own challenges can we transform our belief in ourselves. Only by allowing ourselves to go through this process of reprogramming our neural networks can we create lasting change.

A few months after I had written this chapter, I was at lunch with a friend who told me about the weekend he'd spent with his eight-year old son who had survived his multi-year battle with cancer. He said it was one of the best weekends of his life. After years of chemotherapy his son was finally cancer free. However, his brain has been affected along the way. The chemotherapy had left him with some brain damage in the cerebellum, which is the part of the brain responsible for balance, movement and coordination. Although the chance of the cancer recurring is very slim, the doctors told my friend that his son would never be able perform tasks that require even a basic level of coordination, even something as simple as riding a bike.

As my friend described the joy he felt watching his eight-year old son overcome the odds and ride a bike for the very first time in his life I thought back to my own experience. I had to hold back my tears as he explained that watching his son ride a bike meant more to him than watching his son take his first steps because, unlike when his son learned to walk, he had just witnessed a miracle.

At that moment I became even more convinced how important the catalysts are that transform our belief in who we are and in what we can accomplish. His son wanted to ride that bike so badly and wanted to prove all the people wrong who said he couldn't do it. Something inside him drove him to push forward no matter what. Although my friend looked at it as a sheer act of will, there was something happening in his son at a neurobiological level. The pathways in his son's brain were being reprogrammed as the boy attempted to reach his goal so that neurons started firing in a way that finally allowed him to ride that bike. When I followed up with my friend months later, his son was also taking on other challenges that were allegedly beyond his ability. As with my experience, once his pathways became reprogrammed by overcoming one challenge, his son gained the confidence necessary to do other things that he was told were impossible.

Perhaps you now understand that before you can learn how to believe in yourself, your brain needs to become wired in such a way that you create this belief. But, this is where most people get stuck, and where I fell short in trying to teach people how to believe in themselves during my original TEDx Talk. Neurological studies conclude that if you have not already been wired for success, you can take control of your life and program your brain to be wired this way.[11] It should no longer be a mystery that overcoming pain, suffering and obstacles requires your brain to build up a neural-network programmed for self-belief and self-confidence. But there is a huge difference between knowledge and application. An old saying from boxing is that your coach can't do your sparring for you. To be a champion, you have to put in the work yourself. However, how many people have the opportunity to have these types of experiences? You might go through your entire life and not have the breakthrough experience that will allow you to turn into a person of self-belief. What then?

"We are what we repeatedly do. Excellence, then, is not an act but a habit." - Aristotle

CHAPTER 8

Streaking your way to success

L ife continues to be about the process, yet too many people continuously focus on only results. Yet, nature actually provides a physiological system that can assist you in your quest to rewire your brain to be programmed for success. Rewiring your brain for ultimate success is not a new idea, as many studies show. However, there hasn't been a focus on how to bridge the gap between an undisciplined mind and a mind that is rewired for success. This requires a paradigm shift away from what you may have previously been taught.

General Stanley McChrystal was recounting how the U.S. military had to change a centuries long paradigm of military structuring to fight Al Qaida. Not only did the U.S. military have to change their war strategy but had to continue to change it in the face of new challenges that Al Qaida presented because of their complex system of leadership and hierarchy. Because Al Qaida did not have a traditional system of leadership, it was impossible to target any one leader specifically to disrupt their system. They operated like a colony that could automatically replace old leaders in an instant, based on circumstance. It was like fighting against the mythological creature Hydra. When you cut off one head, two would grow back to replace it. From his experience he concluded that complex problems need to be confronted in ways that are "discerning, real-time, responsive, and adaptive."[12] He developed an entirely new strategy that went against hundreds of years of military thought because he understood that to defeat terrorists, we had to learn how we could beat them at their own game.

People who are struggling to succeed are fighting a war as well. They are fighting against their current programming and need to focus on changing that first, before they are able to follow through with any motivational program. Like using traditional military tactics to fight a war against an enemy who has changed the rules of war, motivational thought has not adapted to understand and how to affect real change for those who haven't already been wired for success. Instead, motivational material is geared to help people who already have the ability to become successful but need some coaching to get to the next level. It reaches people who already have the tools to succeed and just need a bit of structure to get them moving towards their goals.

What about the rest? What about the people who aren't pre-wired for success or haven't had that life altering experience that rewired them for success? Because I think that each person should have a chance to be successful, I began researching the human incentive-reward system and concluded that we are fighting against our own biological programming when we focus on long-term goals. Therefore, we must rewire our brains so that reaching those goals is in-line with our pre-programmed system. Instead of fighting against our own biological structures, why not get on the same team with them?

One day, completely accidentally, I found the answer. It is streaking.

You may be asking yourself, "What on Earth does streaking have to do with success, and why would I use it?" You'll be relieved to know that it doesn't involve stripping down to your birthday suit and running through the streets naked. Instead, it's based on the premise that, if you want to be successful, each activity you undertake should be a step in the direction towards that ultimate goal that you define as success. This applies to any type of learning, including learning how to believe in yourself or building self-confidence. Streaking your way to success involves structuring your daily activities in such a way that you reward yourself for completing simple tasks while you are moving towards some larger vision. You will ultimately reach the goals you have set for yourself because of the cumulative effect of your activity. However, you won't lose motivation along the way to your goal because of the mechanism that operates when creating a streak. Streaking can be such a strong force and utilizing streaking can ultimately help you create the belief you need to follow through with all the coaching and motivation you receive. Before I explain the mechanism and the psychological and physiological elements associated with streaking, let me first give you the backstory behind the concept of a streak.

The concept of streaking your way to success was inspired by my teenage daughter, who couldn't break herself away from social media. As with many teens, my wife and I had to limit our daughter's phone use or she would spend every waking moment either watching YouTube videos of other people acting as if their lives were a never-ending party, taking silly pictures of herself and sending them to her friends, or using one of the many communication Apps available to reach out to her friends. Because of this obsession, my wife and I had to set some parameters. Our daughter had up until 10:00pm to use her phone before it was taken away for the evening, and then she would get it back upon waking the next morning. Some nights, her phone would be given over to her mother willingly. However, on other nights, it became a battle.

These battles began in a very consistent manner, with my daughter screaming, "No, you can't take my phone away until I get all my streaks done!" At the time, one of my goals in life had been to avoid social media as much as possible, so I didn't quite understand what she was referring to. Also, practically anyone who has a teenage daughter doesn't want to hear the words "streak" and "social media" used in the same sentence. Therefore, I found myself having to ask her if she could explain herself. My daughter let me know that every time you make contact with one of your friends through one of the various social media channels you are using, a log is kept of who you contacted and then who has contacted you back. If you contact someone and they contact you back, you now have started a streak. A streak must be built on mutual contact. The more days in a row you can make contact with each other, the longer the streak lasts and there is huge pride that accompanies a long streak.

This seemed rather silly to me. However, I soon learned that keeping streaks is actually very difficult, especially because of all the obstacles that can get in the way. Friends may be on phone restriction because they got in trouble, or they may be out of range of cellular service because they are traveling, or they may have lost their phone, or (cruelties of all cruelties) perhaps they may be upset with you and don't reply to your message on purpose. For those who aren't aware, that's called Ghosting and can be thought of as a fate worse than death in the social media world because you're being completely ignored by someone who is supposed to care about you. In each of the above-mentioned cases, the streak is then at extreme risk to end. To a teenager, this can be devastating!

Apparently, some of these streaks can last for years. Some even last through break-ups. That's right. The streak can outlive the relationship. After all, why let a break-up get in the way of a good streak? But, one slight mishap, and a streak may be forfeited forever. The number of streaks you have, along with their length, becomes a badge of honor amongst peers and gives the streak owners social media bragging rights. Long streaks with many people apparently are a barometer of popularity and give a teenager a lot of clout. My daughter's streaks were so important to her, that she would rather have her car taken away or be put on restriction than miss the opportunity to make sure all her streaks were intact on any given day. Very often, the late evening hours become the final opportunity for desperate streak-keeping teenagers to give it that one last shot to make sure that everything is status quo in social media streak world. Taking the phone away prematurely from a streak-hungry teenager is like wrestling the tiara out of a mistakenly crowned pageant runner-up. But why?

There is actually a neurological explanation behind the addiction to social media streaks, which is strangely similar to the addiction to sex, cocaine and running five miles. A study done at Harvard University in 2012 by Diana Tamir et al found that people often become addicted to social media platforms because the act of disclosing information about oneself activates the same part of the brain that is associated with the sensation of pleasure.[13] This pleasure center is the same center that is activated when we are eating food, getting money and having sex. Although, not as powerful of a sensation as having sex, there is still a tremendous amount of pleasure derived and it appears to be at an intrinsic level. But what would cause this pleasure and how is it affirmed through the use of social media?

Corroborative evidence across multiple sources, including the findings of Lauren E. Sherman et al in their 2016 study found that getting positive feedback on social media results in a surge of dopamine and activated the same circuits in the brain that are activated by eating chocolate or winning money.[14] *Psychology Today* defines dopamine as a neurotransmitter, one of the chemicals that is responsible for transmitting signals in between the nerve cells (neurons) of the brain.[15] Dopamine neurons become activated when something good happens unexpectedly, such as the sudden availability of food. Most recreational drugs, like cocaine, cause the release of dopamine and this is thought to contribute to their addictive properties. Research indicates that the strength of this dopamine rush drops as cocaine use is increased over time, leading to heightened frequency of use, which ultimately is what leads to the addiction. Dopamine has been found to be the precursor to our incentive-reward system, signaling to us that we are approaching a pleasurable experience. These effects lead us to an endless loop of pleasure-seeking behavior.[16] Whether it's sex, drugs or social media streaks, we do not seek the actual activity, but are seeking the dopamine rush we get right before the onset of a desired activity. Studies have shown that the pull of dopamine is so strong activities like tweeting on Twitter are harder for people to resist than cigarettes and alcohol.[17]

A release of dopamine leads our brains to learn that the rewards we seek feel good, so that we want to seek after them again.[18] In addition to drug use, sex and winning an unexpected prize; we are also rewarded with a surge of dopamine when we are involved in activities such as exercising, competing and winning, or surviving a harrowing experience. In each case, the dopamine rush that follows is nature's way of rewarding us physiologically after certain types of behavior. It can be thought of as the neurochemical Pavlovian Response.[19] Intuitively, the larger the reward, the larger the rush. However, regardless of the size of the reward, drugs like cocaine or social validation through "likes" on social media, are both ways for humans to bypass any actual need to be face-to-face or to have human contact by causing the brain to synthesize dopamine as our reward.

What can we learn from all this discussion about social media, cocaine and dopamine -and- how much does all of this discussion relate to success? Surprisingly, a lot.

Since dopamine is the chemical that makes us feel happy, we naturally crave it. Biologically, when we do something pleasurable, our reward is a surge of dopamine in the pleasure system of the brain. When something is pleasurable, we want more because we like the feeling that dopamine creates. Therefore, anything we do that creates this feeling will lead us to want to continue doing it. What I have described is not new science, but the explanation of pleasure-seeking behavior by human beings. When we get a "like" on one of our social media postings we get a surge of dopamine. The more "likes," the more dopamine, and the more we seek more "likes." Sounds a lot like an addiction, doesn't it?

Furthermore, the more valuable the "like," the bigger the surge of dopamine. When we have a popular or, even more impressively, a famous person "like" something we post; the social validation of that individual validating us trumps the value of a random person liking something we posted. Regardless of its origination, we crave massive amounts of validation on social media and receive it through both quantity and quality. These two forms of feedback join together like peanut butter and jelly to provide social media positive feedback leading to higher levels of dopamine and a much happier social media life. Understanding the value of each social media interaction helps us understand the power of streaks.

Unlike a simple "like," a streak has a cumulative power that can influence action. Additionally, higher levels of happiness are reached the longer the streak lasts, and the more important the person is that the streak is with. This is how the addiction forms. Streaks continue to grow more valuable the longer they become. I've seen my teenage daughter frantically getting on the phone to track someone down as midnight draws near to keep a streak alive. It becomes a feverish quest to maintain the streak, because failure would lead to misery. Experiencing too many failed streaks can actually lead to depression.

Understanding this concept of addiction to streaks led me to explore how I could create streaks in my own life, outside of social media, and instead streak towards my goals. For me, it started with something physical, like working out every day. Eventually that morphed into multiple streaks that now have me addicted. Every morning when I work out, I place a number by the date of that day's workout log to let me know how many days in a row I've worked out. At the time of this writing, I was up to 639 days in a row. At this point, I can't stop. Imagine having to start that streak over again! That would be nearly two years of work down the drain. The habit literally drives me to make sure that rain or shine, in sickness or in health, that I complete my morning workout.

I'm now addicted to the activities that lead to my goals and my goals take care of themselves. Where most motivational programs are designed to get you pumped up with a bunch of positive energy and a "go hunt your prey" attitude, they neglect to teach you how you can actually reprogram your brain to follow through on the activities you need to accomplish to reach the goals that have you so motivated. Additionally, the motivation doesn't tap into the psychology needed behind creating activity when you don't feel like it. It's one thing to say that you need to conquer your goals by doing things even when you don't feel like it. But, it's an entirely different effect when you teach someone how to actually program themselves to do it. Nobody actually feels like completing tasks that are tediously necessary to reach their goals. But successful people grind away at things that they need to do because they are simply wired differently than those who don't. Streaking is how you can actually rewire your brain to think and take action like a successful person does.

Most people don't quite understand that our bodies, including our brains, are made up of electrical signals that cause thought and motion. Whether we are getting up to get a glass of water from the fridge or solving a complex physics problem; our brain fires electric signals across its synapses to cause our thought and movement. From complex to simple, the basic elements are the same. Certain tasks become automatic and are easy to do, others are not. Newton's First Law of Motion says that a body in motion stays in motion and a body at rest stays at rest, which is why momentum plays such a huge part in our lives.[20] You see it when you get into a rhythm, that has been defined as a flow state, when you are in the middle of a project and it starts humming along without much effort.[21] You see it on the football field when one team seems to start playing with ease and steamrolling the other. You even see it in the classroom when someone has studied the material so well that each correct answer rolls into the next and the test grows easier as it progresses.

Isn't it time to finally learn how to actually follow through on all the knowledge regarding achieving success, instead of constantly dreaming it will happen and being disappointed that it doesn't? If you want to be the person that goes beyond dreaming about success and actually achieves it, streaking can be your path. But your first step must be to determine which micro-goals can help you to get your streaking underway.

"Be not afraid of going slowly, be only afraid
of standing still." - Chinese Proverb

CHAPTER 9

Keeping the streaks alive and setting micro-goals

A s you now understand, our incentive-reward system is anchored by the chemical release of dopamine. Immediately preceding the accomplishment of a goal you have set, you experience a rush of dopamine that rewards you for your achievement. This is a simple system, but not optimal for achieving long-term goals. Understand that human activity is really based the upon the fight or flight response.[22] We have an overriding survival instinct designed to reward us when we hunt and/or gather. We get a rush of adrenaline when we need to run, either towards something or away from something. However, this effect is short-term. The reward we get for reaching a short-term goal doesn't differ significantly from one we receive for reaching a long-term goal. Herein lies the problem.

Think about the situation this way. Let's say that you set two goals: The first goal is to wash and wax your car over the weekend and the second goal is to lose 30 pounds in one year. Because our incentive-reward system has no concept of time, you will get about the same rush of dopamine after you wash and wax your car and after you lose 30 pounds. The reward you receive is not commensurate with the effort. Our biological system is still stuck on the short-term reward plan, while the worthwhile goals in life are almost all long-term. Although the rewards for losing 30 pounds are that you are most likely healthier and have an improved appearance, the level of dopamine rush you receive for accomplishing this long-term goal seems anticlimactic. Especially since you could have received about the same dopamine reward for the completion of a weekend project.

Our society seems to have evolved much faster than our biological system. This fact is another reason why people find it so difficult to follow through on long-term goals they've set. There isn't enough reward along the way to make it worthwhile getting to the light at the end of the tunnel. You might just as well watch some TV or go to a ballgame. Neither of these activities are particularly productive, but at least you get rewarded for these activities. Given this biological disconnect between our incentive-reward system and our achievement of long-term goals, it's no wonder that so few people have the ability to reach their goals and dreams.

However, research has shown that there is a small group of people that seem to be genetically pre-programmed to achieve their long-term goals. In the 1960s Stanford professor Walter Mischel completed a study, ultimately finding what is now accepted as one of the most important characteristics we must have for success, but not really answering the question of how we can develop that characteristic if we don't already have it. It was called the Marshmallow Experiment.[23] The set-up and execution of the experiment were both quite simple. A researcher would be in a room with a child, explain to them that they were going to give them a marshmallow, set it down in front of them and then leave the room for fifteen minutes. The researcher would then explain to the child that, after the fifteen-minute period, if they came back and the marshmallow was still there, then the child would be rewarded with a second marshmallow. However, if the marshmallow was no longer there, then the child would not get a second marshmallow. There was no catch and there were no tricks. All the child had to do was decide if they wanted one marshmallow or two marshmallows. The only thing standing in the way of them getting that second marshmallow was time.

What Mischel found was that some children ate the marshmallow as soon as the researcher left the room, some children would squirm in their seat and wiggle uncontrollably until temptation finally got the best of them and eat the marshmallow, and other children exhibited a litany of other antics before they would ultimately give into the temptation and eat the marshmallow. However, a very select few actually managed to endure the entire fifteen minutes and earn that second marshmallow.

The final results to this experiment were not discovered during the experiment itself, but by studying the children who had participated in the experience years after the experiment was complete. In fact, very few conclusions could be made from a kid eating a marshmallow, except that some kids can delay their gratification for one thing they really want if they believe they will get something more at a later time. To complete the experiment, the researchers followed up on the subjects for the next forty years and discovered some pretty surprising results.

The subjects who had earned the second marshmallow because they had delayed their gratification for the full fifteen minutes during the original experiment had better life outcomes than the ones who could not delay their gratification as measured by SAT scores, educational attainment, body mass index, career success, success in relationships, etc. The eventual conclusion of this decades long study was that people who have the ability to delay gratification have a statistically stronger chance of success in life then those who do not. Why? The study didn't actually say. Maybe it's because most people are not able to delay their gratification for the possibility of a future reward because they want the rush of dopamine today. Maybe it's because the people who have the ability to delay gratification don't let their need for an immediate rush of dopamine override their focus on a longer-term goal. Or, maybe it's simply that there are very few people who are actually wired for success.

Why, then, can so few people actually delay short-term desire for immediate gratification in exchange for achieving a much better long-term goal? It's the same reason that we historically have only about a seven percent savings rate in the United States, that credit card debt is typically greater than the money we have in the bank, and that car payments are quite often much too large compared to the amount of money we make. It's no wonder most people alive today won't have enough money to retire; they just can't help spending money today instead of saving it for the future. What about the people who go on endless diets, fail to follow an exercise program they started and gain back any weight they may lost during the process? The list of people who fail to reach their goals has been a pervasive part of the human condition. Although there are many more examples, I hope that you understand that to change our circumstances, we need to change ourselves. To change ourselves, we need to reprogram our neural pathways. To reprogram our neural pathways, we need to consistently repeat the activities that we want to eventually become habits.

We can do all this by beginning a micro-goal strategy, that ultimately acts in conjunction with streaks. Learning this method of goal setting and tracking provides the ability to visualize a goal, set up an action plan designed to reach that goal and then actually follow through on that action plan!

You may be wondering how we can change our behavior to create new habits that will rewire us for success if we are one of those undisciplined souls who can't delay gratification. Setting up streaks that are attached to the smallest incremental steps taken to reach our goals is the answer. Let's call these small incremental steps "micro-goals." Because we biologically seek the rush of dopamine to make us happy and can't wait long stretches between doses, we need to fill each day with the opportunity to experience that dopamine. The mechanics behind setting ourselves up for success through small surges of happiness is not too complex and can be quite addictive once you start. Instead of becoming addicted to unhealthy activities, why not become addicted to whatever can move you towards an ultimately successful life filled with joy, peace and success? Yes, you can become quite addicted to success if you understand how to set yourself up for it.

Micro-goal setting works because we really need to get rewarded with small steps along the way when we are marching toward a larger goal. The best thing about streaking is that the dopamine rush we crave comes to us day-after-day and we eventually stop relying on it for our sense of accomplishment. Instead, we become proud of the streak as we become addicted to the streak itself and the activity becomes a means to an end. Then, the streak turns into a habit, that becomes ever easier to continue. Finally, the activity associated with your micro-goal and the actual act of keeping track of the streak are the actions that help bridge the gap between an activity and a habit.

Additionally, when you keep track of the streak that is attached to your micro-goal you are programming the neurons in your brain to shift from relying on dopamine to help you follow through on a written activity and, instead, turning the activity into a subconscious act. This is the step that has been missing in motivational literature. Again, how can you start with belief in yourself if you don't already have it? How can you "embrace the grind" and challenge yourself by coming out the other side of suffering if you weren't born with that spirit or haven't experienced that conquering of suffering in your life? Finally, how can you discipline yourself to do the activities of waking up early, never taking no for an answer, and working until the job is done instead of working until you are tired if you don't have that inner voice that drives you to do these things? The answer is that you just cannot do it. You can't simply wake up one day and say that your life is going to change, unless you have gone through something that is life changing. Even then, if the life changing event isn't strong enough to reprogram you for success, any change will be impermanent. However, when you are engaged in the activity of tracking your micro-goals, the connections in your brain that build a habit for that activity begin to grow stronger because of the neurons that have to fire in a specific pattern when you are involved in the activity. This is the part of the brain that will eventually allow the micro-goal to become a habit.

Furthermore, when you physically write down a number next to your micro-goal, here is what occurs at the neurobiological level: You get a rush of dopamine in anticipation of writing the number down. It sounds likes it's a bit too simplistic and maybe even a bit silly. But, getting ready to write a number by your micro-goal is a lot like getting ready to eat a piece of chocolate. The pleasure centers of your brain are activating, and a slight feeling of happiness comes over you. Therefore, the mixture of daily micro-goal accomplishment added to the physical act of keeping track of the streak in a streak journal is the recipe to your success cocktail. This is worth repeating because it's so important. Keeping track of your streak might be the most important step because looking forward to writing that number down after you reach your micro-goal is what produces the dopamine. Remember, looking forward to something is why we get that dopamine rush, not actually completing the action. So, looking forward to the physical act of keeping track of the streak is what will keep you going day after day.

You now possess all you need to march forward and reprogram your brain for success. So many phenomenal motivational and self-help programs exist that could help you chart your way towards success, but I don't recommend one over another. I have found that the best program is the one that works for you. All have something great to offer and they each speak with a different tone. The one that speaks to you, may not be the one that speaks to me. However, what is certain is that unless you have reprogrammed your mind to have a strong belief in yourself, none of the programs will work. Once you have that belief, any of them will. It's not the program that is necessarily special, it's that you are special. Now that you've learned the mechanics behind creating an amazing belief in yourself, you can begin the next chapter in your life. This will be the chapter that starts your journey to reaching your goals and achieving the success you dream of.

"Don't judge each day by the harvest you reap, but by the seeds you plant." - Robert Louis Stevenson

CHAPTER 10

Putting streaks into action

Let's paint a simple picture that allows someone to work towards a chosen goal, with very little focus on the goal itself and more focus on the daily steps it takes to reach the goal. Imagine wanting to lose weight although every diet and exercise plan you've tried has failed you. Why not set yourself up for a rewarding surge of happiness at the end of each day, and maybe even throughout each day, as you use the concept of streaks in your micro-goal planning. Mind you, I am not a doctor. As with any diet or exercise program you embark on, it is recommended that you seek the help of a doctor or trained professional to make sure that your progress is monitored properly. My goal in this chapter is not to give you medical advice, but to teach you how to use the concept of streaking so you can, not only, follow through on a program designed to help you lose weight in a healthy manner but also reprogram your brain to help you keep it off. The following pages provide a step-by-step example of how to build your micro-goals toward losing weight in a way that will allow you to focus on small daily goals, fulfill your need for the reward of a dopamine surge, and eventually develop habits giving you the ability to keep the weight off. However, this example can be used to break any long-term goal down into micro-goals in order to achieve the success you seek.

To get started, calculate your target weight and the time in which you think it will take you will reach it. You can do this realistically by estimate, or by simply talking to a nutritionist who can give you a rough guesstimate of how much weight you can safely lose over a given period of time. You can also talk to a fitness trainer to understand what type of exercise program is best for you. Alternatively, there are plenty of free Apps available in the iTunes or Android App Store that can help you with your diet. The principle is that you have to put some effort into figuring out what your specific daily micro-goal should be in order to work toward losing the weight. If you don't have the energy to go through all this effort, at the very least, cut some sugar out of your diet and go for a walk every day. Now, you have two micro-goals to start with. However, I suggest you expend the energy so you can set the best micro-goals possible.

Once you understand the relationship between time and weight loss, set a target. For example; if you can safely lose five pounds a month and you want to lose thirty-five pounds, then it will take you seven months to lose the weight (7 x 5 = 35). If it's currently May 3rd, then you'll write down your goal in a journal or on a flashcard in the present tense by writing, "I lost 35 pounds of fat over the past seven months, it's now December 3rd and I feel great!" If you don't know already, your brain really doesn't understand time. Therefore, goals are best realized if they are written in the present tense. Is this part of goal setting mandatory? No, it's not. But, because of the way the brain works, you can use tricks like this to give yourself the best shot at success.

Now determine how much protein, fat and carbohydrates (in the proper balance) you would need to eat each day in order to lose five pounds in a month. Let's say that you weigh 235 pounds and your target is to lose five pounds over the next month. Calculate how much a 230-pound person needs to eat and set up a specific plan to eat that amount. Again, if the calculation feels too complicated, work with a nutritionist or use an App to help you come up with the number. If you need to keep it simple, you can always start by eating about five percent less than you normally consume each day over the course of the next month. The objective is to define a reasonable target for your daily caloric intake.

Every day that you reach the target calorie intake, log that achievement in your streak journal. Every day that you exercise, log that achievement in your streak journal. Every day that you don't eat a candy bar or other sugary snack, log that in your streak journal. Guess what? You just got a surge of dopamine each time you are about to add another day to your streak. Now, each day that you continue to eat the proper amount of food and log that accomplishment, more dopamine! Each day that you exercise based on your defined plan and log that accomplishment, more dopamine. Each day that you avoid eating a candy bar and log that accomplishment, even more dopamine. This approach is so important to understand. Your goal is no longer to lose weight. Instead, your micro-goals are to eat a defined amount of calories today, exercise today according to your plan and avoid eating a candy bar today. That's it. You don't have any long-term goals to focus on. You are only focusing on today. Your micro-goals become very easy to reach and you get rewarded each day for reaching them when you physically log your accomplishments in a streak journal. Keeping track of how many days in a row you reach your micro-goal is what provides you with a dopamine rush and rewards you on a daily basis. Imagine if you were building a wall and each day you got paid after laying three bricks. You would stop caring about the completion of the wall because your job is no longer to build a wall that will be completed sometime in the future, but to lay three bricks today. So, lay your bricks, get paid and move on.

After a few days, your desire to continue the streaks you started and the little surges of dopamine you are receiving will keep you going. Here is some key advice. Don't even step on the scale because it doesn't matter. Remember, losing weight is not a micro-goal, but a result of you achieving your micro-goals for thirty days in a row. The goal of losing the five pounds takes care of itself, and you only have to focus on your daily micro-goals instead of the end result.

After the thirty days, step on the scale and there is a very good chance that you now weigh 230 pounds or less. If you do, congratulations! If you do not, congratulations! Remember, your goal was not to lose five pounds. Your goals were to complete your daily micro-goals and to log their completion so you can get a rush of dopamine with each streak you build. Regardless of the outcome, continue on with your streak of micro-goals because the logging of the accomplishment of the micro-goal is what is important. Think about it this way: If you want to row across the English Channel and it takes 10,000 strokes to do it, your goal is not to complete 10,000 strokes. Your goal is to complete one stroke. That's it. To reach your goal, you don't count to 10,000. Instead, count to 1…you just have to do it 10,000 times. How you approach this monumental task will make all the difference in the world because counting to 1 is easy, but counting to 10,000 is hard.

Now it's important to understand that, whether or not you lost five pounds, it's time to recalculate your goal for the next month by eating what a 225-pound person would eat and continue the streaks of your micro-goals. Don't reset the streaks to start over again in the new month. Continue the old ones. If you maintain your streaking throughout this process, you will have a streak of over 210 days in a row by the time you get to December 3rd and you should be at your target weight. You may lose five pounds one month, none the next month and lose seven pounds the next. That's okay. Losing weight is not an exact science, but instead is an experiment you conduct with yourself until you figure out what works. Think about it logically. If you continue to lower your food intake every single month, avoid sweets and exercise for 210 days in a row, the chances are very high that you will have lost the weight.

Additionally, because you have been rewarded each day, you are getting these little surges of dopamine and you are living your life one day at a time. By the time December 3rd arrives, even if you are not exactly at your target weight, you will have accomplished something even better. You will have developed a habit of eating well and exercising and your brain will have been rewired to continue. You have now changed your lifestyle and are actually eating like a healthy person who weighs what you want to weigh and exercises to stay healthy. Your entire mindset has now shifted to focus on the activity and not the result. By the way, this is exactly what successful people do. Congratulations! You have taken a huge step toward getting rewired for success.

At this point, if you are not exactly at your target weight, you still should continue building on your streak. You will eventually get to your target weight as long as you continue to lower your calorie intake at the end of each month, avoid sweets and continue to exercise. It might take you ten months, or it may happen in five, or it even might happen in a year-and-a-half. Regardless of when you reach your target weight you will get rewarded each day with a surge of dopamine, be happy along the way because of this short-term reward, and achieve the reward of being who you wanted to become. Additionally, you now know exactly what your caloric intake should consist of each day because you have slowly reached that point in a healthy manner and will be able to maintain these new eating and exercise habits.

Now that you are at your target weight, you can stay there because the major challenge of losing weight is keeping it off after you've lost it and you have actually developed a habit that won't go away unless you let it. So, don't end your streak. Since you are at your target weight and you are eating the proper amount of calories to maintain your target weight, your new micro-goal now becomes to maintain this streak for the rest of your life. Each day that you add to the streak, you become more invested in it and the chance that you end it is very small. I have streaks that are well over four years long. It could be 11:30pm on a Sunday night and all I want to do is go to bed, but I will add to one of those streaks no matter what. This is what is called being addicted to success. It starts off as biological addiction to dopamine, moves into an obsession with a micro-goal setting and ends up as a real habit that is anchored to goal-driven activity.

"Happiness is not found in pleasure, instead happiness is found in victory." - Zig Ziglar

CHAPTER 11

What to do when the dopamine rush fades

When you first start tracking your daily goals and logging your streaks, you are conscientiously completing tasks you have set for yourself. As a result, you get that surge of dopamine you crave. But, further along, the dopamine rush you get from your streaks begins to diminish. It's still occurring, but not as much as when you first started. However, when you start a new streak, the surge of dopamine you receive once again heightens as you begin tracking the streak. For that reason, it's a good idea to begin another streak for a different micro-goal, and then yet another, until you have multiple streaks going simultaneously. If you do this, you will continue to experience the benefits of the dopamine rush on any given day. This will help you continue making progress. Basically, streaking with clusters of micro-goals keeps your streaks alive.

Inevitably, you may get to the point where you can't maintain any more streaks without risking becoming overwhelmed with too much activity and becoming ineffective. What then? You'll likely notice that your will to succeed will take over, because you won't want to turn back and have to start over again. You might be twenty or thirty days into a streak and you simply won't want to go back to zero or you'll feel like you've failed. This is the point at which you are no longer being driven by dopamine, which is a temporary drive. Instead, you will have graduated into being driven by grit, which is lasting. Congratulations! You are in the initial phase of being reprogrammed for success. Somewhere on your path towards your goals, your drive has evolved to the level that overachievers possess. You are now acting because you are driven by a big voice inside that will not let you fail and makes you push through your challenges, no matter what the sacrifice. At this point you will have matured to attain the level of an accomplishment mindset because you no longer have to rely on the fleeting happiness of a dopamine rush.

Ideally, by now, you can move into a state of joy, which can be described as a permanent happiness. Remember, happiness is fleeting because it's a temporary state. In contrast, joy is a state that you carry with you each moment of every day. You could be going through some rough times where it's tough to be happy, but you can still be joyful. Things might not be going according to plan, but you can still be joyful. Isn't this what we are inevitably searching for? Isn't this the level of consciousness that we seek to achieve? Once you are at this level, you've actually created belief in yourself and nothing can shake your resolve. Now you can truly start on your road to success because you are no longer trapped with an endless search for happiness and, instead, you can live a life of fulfillment and joy while in pursuit of your ultimate desires.

But, what happens when you miss a micro-goal and your streak ends? It is imperative that you understand how to deal with this because, unless you are perfect, it will happen and it can completely derail you from achieving your goals.

When your streak ends because you "messed up," you will most likely get upset with yourself and beat yourself up about it. Good! This feeling shows that you are committed and now are frustrated that you let yourself down. However, the best response is that you must simply let it go. That's right, just move on and start a new streak. Please understand, that here is the point that separates those who can ultimately succeed from those who will not. In their work on studying how humans cope with regrets, researches Bauer and Wrosch found that, "Moving on and being able to maintain good emotional well-being depends greatly on an individual's opportunity to correct the cause of their regrets."[24] Therefore, as soon as you feel that you have a regret, the ability to correct the cause is crucial for your ultimate success. Even if it means forgiving yourself for a failure, you can learn from your failure and start with a new challenge. It's within the depths of our own regrets that we must battle ourselves, conquer that regret and continue to fight on! This is where our true character is revealed.

When you have regret associated with missing one of your micro-goals, leading to the end of a streak, you must determine the cause. Then, you can correct the mistake and move forward immediately. This wisdom is just like that which is given in the old saying, "If you fall off a horse, get right back on." Here is one example based on one of my own botched streaks. It isn't an example of an earth-shattering micro-goal that I had, and its failure wasn't an epic blow to my success. Instead, it's meant to illustrate that all of us have our personal goals and it's entirely okay to go for them regardless of how big or small they may seem.

There was a point in my life that I could do one hundred consecutive push-ups. It had taken me years to reach this level of fitness and I've spent many years being proud of being in great shape. Then, one day in Jiu Jitsu, I tore my right pectoral muscle. Luckily, it was only a partial tear and the doctor said that surgery was only optional because whether I had the surgery or not, my strength would never be back to one hundred percent of what it was before the injury. My choices were to have the surgery and live with a small scar for the rest of my life, or to not have the surgery and live with a small divot in my chest for the rest of my life. Because I'd had seven surgeries already in my life, I decided to live with the divot rather than go through yet another surgery.

Having many injuries in the past, I knew how to rehabilitate myself. The rehab was long and painful, but I fought through it every day. Not only was my right pectoral muscle very weak, but it ached most of the time, especially when I worked out. After many years I managed to slowly rebuild the strength in my chest and had become as strong as I had been before the injury. However, for some reason the level of my endurance was inadequate because I could only complete about twenty push-ups. One day I decided that I wanted to be able to complete one hundred consecutive push-ups again. Therefore, my micro-goal became to complete the maximum number of strict push-ups (all the way up and then all the way down) I could do each night before I went to bed. In my streak journal, I would simply write down the amount of repetitions I did and for how many nights in a row I had done them. Every night I looked forward to doing as many push-ups as I could so that I could get my little shot of dopamine as I got to chart my push-up streak for the day.

After sixty days, my maximum was only thirty repetitions and I started to realize that this goal of one hundred consecutive push-ups might take much longer than I had anticipated. But, that's the beauty of micro-goals. Not knowing exactly how long it would take to get to one hundred, my goal had nothing to do with the eventual number. If it took three months, great! If it took three years, great! The goal was the daily activity itself. Each day, I had to remind myself that my goal wasn't the one hundred push-ups. Instead, my goal was to do the maximum number of push-ups I could do that day. That's it. Then, since tomorrow would become another new day the minute I woke up, all I needed to do was focus on that one goal on that one day. Eventually, I knew that I would reach my ultimate goal. Focusing on doing as many push-ups as I can do today is such a simple goal. Whereas thinking of the many months (maybe years) it would take to get to one hundred is just too overwhelming. My micro-goal was set, I was motivated and it became one of my easier daily tasks.

Then, on day sixty-seven something happened. I completely forgot to do my push-ups. There was no reason that I could point to, nothing that happened that caused me to be unable to do it and there was no good excuse. I simply forgot. Of course, because I'm hard on myself, I was quite angry that I had forgotten my push-ups. It really bothered me. But, then, the words of Bauer and Wrosch started ringing in my ears, I got past my disappointment and understood the cause of missing my micro-goal. I was tracking the completion of my nightly push-ups the next morning but, I wasn't checking my list at night. This missed detail inevitably led to a missed day of push-ups. So, I immediately did two things: First, I switched my push-up routine to the morning so that I never had to deal with a midnight bout of push-ups (which had happened on more than one occasion). Second, I started checking my list of streaks before I went to bed to make sure I hadn't missed that one or any others. My problem had now been solved because I analyzed the cause, addressed it and moved on. Admittedly, I was still upset with myself. But it didn't stop me from starting a new streak and forging ahead each morning with a set of push-ups to start the day.

No micro-goal is really much more challenging than doing daily push-ups. How do you think I wrote this book? I applied the same micro-goal and streak strategy. I committed to writing fifteen minutes each day, no matter what. If my writing time lasted longer, then more pages were written. If I had writer's block, then almost nothing was written. However, regardless of how I felt on any given day, the minimum requirement was fifteen minutes. Whether you want to write a book, do one hundred push-ups or save $5 million for retirement, the steps to attain your goal are exactly the same. Simply state your goal, attach micro-goals that will move you towards that goal, and finally attach the micro-goal to a streak. You will then have the advantage of using the incentive-reward system as it has been designed because you will seek rewards for the short-term steps taken, and this will allow you to reach your long-term destination.

"Documenting little details of your everyday life becomes a celebration of who you are." - Carolyn V. Hamilton

CHAPTER 12

How to keep track of your streaks

We know that momentum is our friend. But, how do we create it? The answer is through streaks and micro-goals. All you have to do is pick something you wish to accomplish and design a streak around it by clearly defining your micro-goal. Every time that you complete that activity, write a number in a streak journal. My suggestion is that you keep a physical journal and write the number next to the accomplished micro-goal in long-hand, with an actual pen. Why this suggestion? Because there is a brain-body connection that is made when you physically write something, as opposed to typing it. Writing the number actually engrains the activity into your brain and you will look forward to the physical act of writing your entry. This increases the surge of dopamine you receive.

Obviously, none of this strategy works if you don't have the discipline to write down your goals, chart a course toward reaching your goals, and then outline daily steps needed to navigate this course. The promise of starting streaking was never that it would be easy, just that it is based on science and capitalizes on the way the brain works. Realize that the hardest part of the journey is the first step. Think about the launching of a rocket ship. It's estimated that the Saturn V rocket that was used for the Apollo space missions expelled fifty-five percent of its total fuel and energy within the first forty-two miles of a 240,000 mile journey.[25] However, like the momentum that develops after the launch of a rocket ship, once you begin your streaks, nature will take over and you will achieve the same momentum. Each day you will see that streak grow and it slowly becomes more of an addiction. You will become like my teenage daughter seeking validation through her mounting social media streaks and literally throw a fit if you can't complete the activity that keeps your streak alive.

There have been times when circumstances didn't allow me to reach one of my daily streaks. For instance, when it's 11:30pm and I'm dead tired. In the past, I would have just gone to bed and saved the task I needed to accomplish to move towards my goal for the next day. But, not anymore because streaks are involved. I will stay up and make sure that I get every last streak done because I don't want to see any of them go back to zero. That would be tremendously deflating.

Gradually, streaks begin to own you and they become an addiction. But, in a very positive way. They dictate your activity to a point when you reach one of your goals, you immediately want to add in another one because you want to replace that streak. Why label addiction as bad, when it can lead to tremendous success in your life if you learn to use it properly? Choose not to be addicted to anything that will tear you down, but only to what can build you up.

Although a journey of a thousand miles begins with the first step, it often it ends by the fifth. We often start on projects that may take years to accomplish and these get tossed aside like yesterday's news because we don't have the discipline to follow through with them. Lack of discipline is what we tend to attribute our shortcomings to.

In my opinion, it's not necessarily the lack of discipline that makes us stop from following through. I believe that we stop because there is a disconnect between a long-term goal and a short-term reward for taking a step toward that goal. Small steps that you take along the way are what build the bridge to fill that gap. It's only when we start to find ample reward for each of these steps that we can program ourselves to persevere towards the goals we have set for ourselves.

If you set a goal that will take two years to accomplish, there is little reward for moving towards that goal and motivation to reach that goal typically lasts for only a short period of time. Even a month or two of movement towards such a goal makes such a small dent in the overall task that the most disciplined person can easily lose interest. You can only watch so many motivational speeches on YouTube telling you to keep charging up your mountain of challenges, or to be the lion that you are meant to be, but at some point you will most likely give up. However, if you begin a streak, once you are in it for about thirty days, it will be hard to turn back. Imagine if you are 503 days into your streak. What are the chances you will quit then? Very small. Using the science behind creating positive addictions through streaking can help you accomplish quality long-term goals that can lead to a much brighter and bigger future because you get rewarded for the small steps taken along the way.

As with cocaine or sex, that need to continue in greater amounts to produce the same dopamine rush, a greater number of streaks are also required. What is then needed is for you to create more streaks across more activities, and for the length of your streaks to grow. New habits are being formed during this streaking process and the neurons in your brain begin to fire in a very specific pattern as you get deeper into a streak. You are imprinting the actual activities that you have committed to in the streak, and each day it gets easier for the brain to fire in the learned sequence. Furthermore, this pattern building phenomenon eventually becomes easier for the brain to recall and recreate each time you take on a new task. Therefore, the more you learn to build one habit, the easier it becomes to build other habits.

Using streaks can help you accomplish one more important strength. That is the development of grit. Grit is the illusive personality trait that high achievers possess. It's the same trait that allows people to continue studying when all they want to do is sleep, to continue to run when they want to collapse and continue to move ahead in the face of a challenge when all they want to do is quit. If you aren't born with grit, it's almost impossible to develop unless you go through some experience that changes the way you think. But, what if you never come across such an experience? Or, what if you do, and can't conquer the obstacle facing you? Are you destined to continue falling short of your goals, dreams and aspirations? Luckily, no. You can develop grit through streaking. That's right! When you commit yourself to a streak, the process itself can lead to the development of grit.

Why does this occur? First, the longer a streak lasts, the less dopamine rush you receive with each passing day. However, this isn't necessarily bad. On the contrary, it's necessary. What started as a biologically driven chemical addiction begins to morph into a habit because you start becoming addicted to the actual streak instead of to the feeling you obtain from the dopamine rush. Secondarily, this habit becomes so rooted in your behavior that you can accomplish tasks you need to do, even when you don't feel motivated. Isn't that the mark of someone who has grit? Since grit is the determination to move forward regardless of the circumstances and you have developed a habit that you are addicted to regardless of your mood, then the grit to continue at all costs simply becomes the byproduct of this habit. Congratulations! You are now one of the few who is driven to succeed, isn't fooled by moods and continues to move towards goals as if life depended on achieving them. You will behave like a successful top performer who can operate from a state of total self-belief.

If you've read every self-help book on motivation, listened to every guru on the topic and watched every video you can get your hands on but still find yourself falling short, it's not your fault. Although most of the suggestions that you've heard about believing in yourself, about doing small things each day, and about counting backwards from five so you can launch each activity are all great suggestions.[26] But, they don't work unless you have already been wired for success. This becomes a motivational Catch-22: You need to believe in yourself so that you have the ability to take the small steps needed to move towards success, but you need to have the ability to take the small steps needed to move toward success in order to believe in yourself. No wonder most people never get out of the starting blocks!

If you were already born with the "grit" gene, then all the suggestions you've heard for achieving success will work because you have the intrinsic ability to apply them. However, if you don't already have this grit gene built in, you have to create it. The best way to create it is by developing habit forming steaks that trick your brain into producing a dopamine rush for your activity and addict you to the habits that can ultimately lead you to success.

If all else has failed in your life, when it comes to finding success, then it's time for you to streak! Eventually, the dopamine rush linked to streaking will subside and you won't need it anymore. You will reach a point where keeping track of the streak can take a back seat to the true motivation you have developed to complete your daily tasks and to work towards your goals, relying on neither the dopamine nor on the streaks. You will have transformed yourself from someone who needs streaks to keep you motivated towards a goal into someone who is happy simply reaching for the goal. At this moment you will have truly created belief in yourself. You will have developed a spirit of never giving up and will have joined the league of people who are truly successful.

"Consider it pure joy, my brothers and sisters, whenever you face trials of many kinds, because you know that the testing of your faith produces perseverance." - James 1:2

CHAPTER 13

What happens when you lose a streak?

In the course of your journey, you will miss a day in one of your streaks from time to time. How you react to this misstep is more important than the fact that you missed it. If you get too upset and you give up, then it will be very difficult for you to persevere at anything. No one can always be perfect. You must keep in mind that you are a work in progress and are doing the best that you can. The fact that you are one of the few that is actually conscious of doing what it takes to achieve your goals in your life already sets you apart. But, if you give up along the way, you don't give yourself the chance to find out who you could have become.

Losing a streak can lead to a range of emotions, driven by the circumstances behind the loss as well as where you are within the progression of the streak. If a streak ends because you had an unexpected life emergency, something came up in your schedule and you just couldn't make the time or you simply forgot; you must continue on and start a new streak right away. If you don't, then you will form the habit of quitting your streaks and set yourself up to never reach your potential.

I saw this unfortunate effect in the life of one of my close friends. He loved the idea of streaking and wanted to apply it to his life. Things had been going well for him. He had a wonderful wife, a great house, a fulfilling career and was in a satisfying place in his spiritual life. But he felt that he had let his commitment to his health and fitness slide. He wanted to get healthy again. When he was younger, he would run every day and felt that was when he was at his peak. So, he made a deal with himself that he would run every day for one year straight. It sounded like a great plan and he was going to use streaking as his way to help him follow through. However, he made two mistakes. One was when he decided to start his streak and one was how it ended.

He first thought of the running streak in the early fall and decided that his New Year's resolution would be to run one mile each day for 365 days in a row. The mistake he made was that he made his decision in October but was procrastinating from the beginning. "Why not just start your streak today?" I asked him. He responded with some excuse about getting to enjoy the rest of the year. His birthday was approaching, and he wanted to enjoy it without having to stress about running and eating well. Then, Thanksgiving and Christmas followed his birthday, so it would be tough to get through those holidays without slacking a bit. In his mind this streak was going to really challenge his lifestyle, so he wanted to give himself a couple of extra months to continue slacking off before beginning.

This was clearly a mistake because he began to eat more indulgently than he normally would, because he knew he was going to work it off in the coming year. So, he put on some extra unwanted pounds by the time he was ready to start. Additionally, some say that there is nothing as strong as a mind that is made up. The question is, was his mind really made up? If he was really that excited about getting back in shape, why didn't he start that same day? Plus, his logic of waiting to start because of his birthday and holiday schedule was actually illogical. When you think about it, all the same things he was facing in the coming months that caused him to delay his effort would be faced again the following year as well. Regardless of when he chose to start, he had a one-year goal. Therefore, he would never be able to avoid running during his birthday or the holidays. However, this is what people who procrastinate on working towards their goals commonly do and he fell victim to it as well.

It's simple. If you really want to do something, it's best to do it right away. If you don't really want to do something, you'll tend to procrastinate. The infamous business and sales coach, Zig Ziglar, had a great story that illustrated this point very well.[27] He would pose the question, "If your best friend called you up and said that he and his wife were heading to an all-expenses-paid one week vacation to Acapulco, had two extra tickets and wanted to know if you and your spouse could join them, would you say yes?" Well, of course you would, and you would be excited about it. What if the next thing your friend told you was that you had to be ready to leave in twenty-four hours? At that point, wouldn't you look at your to-do list in a whole different light? Most likely, you would make sure that everything you needed to do over the next week was either taken care of, rescheduled or cancelled. You would clearly do everything in your power over the next twenty-four hours to make sure that you were ready to go. Then, Zig would pose another question, "Why can't you work like you were heading to Acapulco in twenty-four hours every day of your life?"

Imagine how productive you would be if you had to have your accomplishments met within the next twenty-four hours. It sounds so exciting, is great advice and when you hear Ziglar explain it it's truly motivational. However, the reason that most people can't follow through with a heightened pace of work every day of their lives in order to reach their goals more quickly is that the incentive of going to Acapulco for free doesn't commonly exist in our daily lives. The reason we can't fool ourselves into creating this sense of excitement each day is because of our human nature and the way our incentive-reward system works. As we've already stated, we are wired to get rewarded for achieving very short-term goals, and not long-term goals. The result is that we get stuck in the trap we have been discussing during this entire book. We are trapped within a system that is wired differently than the system we need to reach our long-term goals, unless we trick the system in such a way that is in-line with our need for short-term rewards. Again, this is why the combination of micro-goals and streaking works so well. This combination simulates short trips to Acapulco every single day and allows us to focus on only our micro-goals, allowing the long-term goals to automatically take care of themselves.

My friend didn't understand this concept at all and fell into the typical "New Year's Resolution" trap. People think that there is some sort of magic that exists when the calendar winds through to another year that will bring a sudden change in their lives. Most New Year's Resolutions don't make it through the end of January because there is no magic. You are the same person you were last year, the year before and the year before that. Not wanting to admit this, my friend eventually started off on his one-mile-a-day journey on New Year's Day. I was actually proud of him because he made it to day eighty before he missed a day. Then, he quit. When I pressed him as to the reason why he didn't continue, his answer showed that he missed the point of the challenge he had started. He said that he was angry with himself that he missed his goal of running a mile-a-day for a year straight. Because he missed a day, he failed at his goal and gave up.

Yes, he did fail at his goal of running one mile-a-day for a year straight. However, he could have used this failure as his fuel and could have started a new streak right away. What he missed is that he still could have run a mile-a-day consecutively for the next year. He didn't have to quit his streak. He was entirely focused on the plan that his goal could only be accomplished from January 1st to December 31st. That is, he substituted his running goal with a calendar goal. Let's contrast that with a simple micro-goal. Imagine if his goal were to run a mile-a-day for one year in a row, regardless of the start date. Then, let's say that his micro-goal was to run one mile today. If he would have missed his micro-goal in this situation, he would simply start his streak over and keep his goal of running a mile-a-day for a year. In this situation, he will again get rewarded for his daily action and will eventually reach his ultimate goal as long as he focuses on what he has to do one day at a time.

But what if he misses a day or two each month? We can agree that this isn't the optimal result and he isn't utilizing the dopamine rush he receives from seeing his streak continue to grow. However, at the end of the calendar year, even if he missed two full days each month, he would have run 341 out of 365 days, which represents 341 miles and a success rate of 93.4%. Again, he failed to run every day for a year. But, wouldn't it be better to come close to accomplishing your goal by continuing to forge ahead even after a failure than to give up and quit? In my opinion, running 341 miles in one year is a whole lot better than running only 80 miles and then quitting.

This example shows us that we don't need to be perfect. We will likely fail along the way to reaching our goals, we will ultimately make mistakes and we will have lapses in judgment. However, we will benefit more if we continue charging after our goals even when we fail because we will be making progress. When we make progress, we are successful. Additionally, chances are there won't be too many failures along the way because the longer you persist in a streak, the stronger the habit surrounding your streak becomes. The longer your streak continues, the more your brain is becoming programmed to accomplish the goals you define and the positive habits you are developing continue to strengthen. If you miss a day during one of your streaks, get right back on your horse and don't beat yourself up too much. Such persistence will give you the best chance at reaching all the goals you've set for yourself and the best chance at ultimate success.

"Give me six hours to chop down a tree and I will spend the first four sharpening the axe." - Abraham Lincoln

CHAPTER 14

Learn how to work smart

We are told that if we outwork our competition then we will achieve success. This maxim is sold to us from the time we are young and, when we work hard and it doesn't lead to the success we seek, we criticize ourselves. Then, we give up and conclude that "things aren't meant to go our way." Or, we buckle down and work even harder, which may not get us where we want to be either. This aspect of life is frustrating. Just because you work hard at something, doesn't mean that you will reach your eventual goals.

You can work hard all day in an attempt to knock down a solid brick wall by leaning on it with all your strength and it will never fall. The wall will continue to stand no matter how much sweat equity you invest. You can show up day-after-day, continue pushing and the result will be the same. The hard work accomplishes absolutely nothing because you aren't working smart. Your useless work won't amount to accomplishing anything but a sore back and is exactly what most people are doing in their own lives. They work tremendously hard and accomplish very little.

Whether it's pushing on a wall all day or pushing a stone up a hill endlessly like Sisyphus, work in and of itself will not lead you to success.[28] Please don't misinterpret what I'm saying because it's critical that you work hard, and I advocate hard work. But, if you are not working efficiently, effectively and with expertise in your craft then you are destined to suffer the fate of being a brick wall pusher. This becomes a life of hard work that greatly lowers your chances of reaching your potential. You are either doing something that you don't have the capacity for, you aren't using the correct tools, or you simply don't yet have the proper knowledge to conquer the task at hand. If you really want to knock down a wall, grab a sledgehammer. Or, better yet, hire someone to do it for you. It's not that you couldn't do it with the proper tools, but you need to decide if your time might be better used elsewhere. The point is that you have to be able to assess your situation correctly to make sure that you are reaching towards goals that align with your talents and for which you have the proper tools.

A great example of someone who understood how to use the tools that he has been given is Mark Cuban, the billionaire who couldn't play basketball but became wealthy enough to purchase a basketball team. Although he loved sports, he knew that he didn't have the genetic gifts to become a professional athlete. It's not that he didn't have the work ethic, it's that he didn't have the athletic talent.[29] However, since an early age, he excelled in two things: hard work and sales. Notice, he had the ability to work hard. In fact, that is one of his self-admitted skills. He has the uncanny ability to work at a level that would crumble most people. But his real talent is that he knows how to apply his efforts in a career that is aligned with his talents. When he was quite young, he attended a stamp show and purchased a stamp at the beginning of the day for $0.25, traded stamps for the entire day and eventually walked out with $50.00 at the end of the day. Although he knew that he wasn't good at sports, this experience helped him realize that he was great at business.

Rather than chase the unreachable dream of becoming a professional athlete, he turned his work-ethic and skills in business into a multi-billion-dollar empire and eventually purchased the Dallas Mavericks professional basketball team. His goal wasn't to become a professional athlete. Instead his goal was to become a billionaire, which is more money than ninety-nine-point-nine percent of even the highest paid professional athletes amass over their careers. His success was achieved by focusing his work ethic in the right direction and pursuing something that was in line with his talents and abilities. Interestingly, I was never really a Mark Cuban fan until I started researching how he became successful. His is an amazing story and his success serves as a great example of someone who figured it out. So, I grew to have respect for Mark Cuban's accomplishments and the process he uses to get results.

Understanding the concept that hard work doesn't guarantee success is one of the hardest pills in life to swallow. Like pushing on a brick wall or working hard on a skill that you will never be great at, the work itself is not going to get you where you wish to go. You must ask yourself each day if the work that you are doing is something that you can become great at and if you are willing to change what you are doing if it's not. Because one of the greatest skills you can develop on your road to success is knowing how to work smart, it sometimes takes a tremendous amount of introspective thought to figure out where you are most talented so you can follow through with this skill. When you work smart you open the door to be more efficient with your time, to do those things that are aligned with your talents and to have a more fulfilling career.

In addition to knowing how to work smart, you have to understand when market conditions change and that what you're successful at today may become an obsolete skill, service or product. Imagine what would have happened to Apple if the company never figured out that they were an entertainment company and that their hardware was simply a delivery system for their music and Application (App) service. Actually, you don't have to imagine too much because that's actually what occurred in the late 1990's before they eventually decided to bring Steve Jobs back to the company he originally founded.[30] Apple had been floundering because the leadership continued to push computers. When Jobs came back to the company, he created the iPod. This innovation changed the way people thought about storing, purchasing and listening to music and led to every other "i" product. Think about how revolutionary the development of this ecosystem was. Jobs isn't just credited with saving Apple, but it's widely thought that he also saved the music industry.[31]

At the time that Jobs returned to Apple, Napster, the free peer-to-peer music sharing service, was sucking the profit out of the entire music industry. Not only were the labels and studios affected, but the artists were getting hurt as well. Steve Jobs went from record label to record label and explained how iTunes works and they fought him tooth and nail, telling him that no one will buy songs for 99 cents and if they do, then no one will buy complete albums. Clearly, they were wrong. If Apple hadn't changed its business model and hadn't focused on the evolution of their company, then we may have never had the smart phone, iTunes, Apple Pay or any of the company's other innovations. There's also a high probability that the music industry would be a shadow of what it is today. This transformation all came from one person understanding that to survive in a market with an evolving consumer, you need to have a company that is willing to change its business model. This innovation at Apple is an example of how important it is to know when to change. But there are also times when change isn't enough and you need to quit and move on, which is what I did after making it through the financial crisis of 2008.

"Strategic quitting is the secret of successful organizations." - Seth Godin

CHAPTER 15

Know when to quit

My partners and I owned an investment company that was formed in the year 2001. We grew it from a fledgling startup into one of the fastest growing investment companies on the west coast. We were in our infancy during the attacks on our country on September 11th, 2001. But we faced the crisis head on and gained a tremendous amount of trust from our clients because we helped get them through this tragedy. We felt as if the stars were aligned because we were willing to combine our strong work ethic with our skillset in a market that was set up for our success.

Our company formed its identity during the recession of the early 2000's by setting ourselves apart through our research and our understanding of global economic trends. As an independent brokerage, we didn't have the ability to invest on the various boards of exchange directly for our clients. Per regulations, we had to have a contractual relationship with a clearing house that did have this ability and could guarantee the transactions we were making on behalf of our clients.[32] We finally hit our stride in May of 2008. After almost a year of negotiation, we partnered with a new firm through which we could clear our business because they had the bandwidth we needed to take our company to the next level. One of the core beliefs we had developed was that if we worked harder than everyone else in the business that our results would speak for themselves and our success would simply be the reward for our efforts. Then, suddenly, our view of success was challenged with the largest financial crisis we had seen in our lifetime.

In 2008, the world entered dark times as the global economy held on for dear life. We were not alone in our suffering, although it often felt as if we were. No matter how hard we worked, the waves of bad news continued to come. Starting in 2007, there was a sub-prime mortgage crisis in the housing market due to the large number of defaults in mortgage debt and the global economy ground to a halt. The S&P 500 plummeted from an intraday high of 1,576.09 on October 11th of 2007 to a low of 666.79 in March of 2009 and didn't completely recover until it surpassed the previous 2007 intraday high, eventually closing at 1,569.19, on March 28th of 2013.[33] Anyone who lived through that time can remember how exhausting it was to watch the stock market plummet for almost a year-and-a-half and felt the effects of the debt crisis seeping into every crack of their lives.

During the initial years of the crisis the revenue coming into our company declined but our overhead remained the same. At that time, even if people were somehow making money in their accounts it was bad for us because they would withdraw it to satisfy some other debt they needed to pay. If they were making money, we were losing revenue. If they were losing money, we were losing revenue. We were stuck in a no-win situation and the only way to survive was to cut costs, renegotiate leases and get lean where we could. While the large U.S. corporations were getting bailed out because they were too big to fail, small businesses like ours needed to fend for themselves. Because we were a private company and lending had seized up, we acted as our own bank and were using our savings to make payroll and to keep the company afloat.

Mike Tyson, who was the youngest heavyweight champion in history, once said that, "everyone has a plan until they get punched in the face." As a martial artist and Jiu Jitsu practitioner, I understood that statement very well in the physical sense. But as a businessman I had never experienced it to that level. Don't get me wrong. I had many challenges in my career as I was building my knowledge base to a level qualifying me to help run a company. But the challenges could always be overcome with more education and more hard work. Additionally, I usually had a plan that I could fall back on. During and after the financial crisis, the plan was to come up with a new plan because even my back-up plan wouldn't have been something I could have depended on. Admittedly, there was a point during these horrible economic times when I felt like a victim. It was so easy to look at what was happening in the world and feel sorry for myself. But that is the point at which the decision was made to do what I have always done since I was that twelve-year old boy doing curls to earn a BMX bike. The decision was made to fight the good fight, no matter what, and start punching back.

Although it took us years to recover, we finally did. It was grueling and there were many sacrifices of time, energy and money. The experience was like doing curls endlessly for five years straight. There were times when it seemed as if there was no light at the end of the tunnel. When that happens in life, your only choice is to kick into a survival mode and continue to move forward. I learned more about my ability to fight through adversity during those five long and painfully difficult years from March of 2008 to March of 2013. I also learned that sometimes what you're fighting for isn't what you really want. After we had restructured the company, I realized that my partners and I were no longer on the same page and clearly had different goals regarding the future direction of our business.

One partner came into the business after 2009 and started to take excessive risk on the portfolios he managed for the company. Although the strategies were designed to outperform market return, the risk was not palatable, and we thought it best to part ways. The exit wasn't as smooth as it could have been because he decided that he would try and take all our business after he left, completely ignoring the agreement we had made. After we filed a lawsuit against him, he agreed to cease and desist, but some damage had already been done.

Another partner came up with a clever scheme to embezzle money through our insurance division by setting up a shell corporation behind our backs and diverting funds that were supposed to come into the company, something that was very difficult to detect. He did this over many months and in small increments, which was both a blessing and a curse. It was a blessing because he only managed to embezzle about $100,000. It was a curse because it took us six months to figure out. We pressed charges, but nothing ever came of it because, in the shadow of a global financial meltdown, the amount he took didn't inspire the authorities to spend too many resources on the case.

My last partner and I just had philosophical differences in the way we wanted to continue to run our business. I wished him no ill will but knew that we could no longer work together. There is a saying that crisis builds character. However, I've come to believe crisis reveals character. For years my partner and I had agreed about most of our business decisions. Looking back, it may have been because the company was doing well, most of our ideas panned out and we were surpassing all our goals. I guess there were kinks in our relationship, but they weren't evident. There was one pivotal moment during the rebuilding phase that tore us apart.

I started doing radio ads for the company on a local talk-radio station and, about six months into it, got the opportunity to be interviewed on Bloomberg Financial Radio. Our head of business development, who was the one that had created the opportunity, wasn't sure what the topic of the interview would be and there was only one day for me to prepare. When he asked Bloomberg what we should do to make sure I was ready, they just told him that I needed to be prepared to discuss the markets. A bit of a wide net, but I was ready to jump into the ocean of financial infotainment because it was a huge opportunity for the company. After many years in the industry, it made sense that I had some key talking points on the general state of the financial market and economy. Additionally, it made sense to have some market-specific data at my fingertips. After many hours of research the night before, and a last minute prep the day of the interview, I felt ready.

For those who don't know, Bloomberg is to the financial industry as the Golden Globes are to the entertainment industry. Insiders and professionals get their information from Bloomberg and it's the financial network that everyone who wants to be taken seriously as a financial analyst wants to be interviewed on. There was a lot of pressure to perform well with an opportunity like this because, if you don't do well you won't get another chance. But, if you do well, being a reoccurring guest on Bloomberg Financial Radio will inevitably lead to other opportunities. Completely prepared, and locked-and-loaded with an extra smattering of notes that were strewn across my desk, the interview went flawlessly. Afterwards, the producers reached out to my director of business development and asked to book me for another interview. He informed them that I have a partner and that we do everything 50/50. So, my partner would like to do the next interview. He assured them that my partner was just as good as I was and that they wouldn't regret it.

My partner was extremely nervous of speaking in public. This seemed odd, because he was a very likable, confident and witty person. But, for some reason, his charisma did not come across when he spoke in front of a large audience. Once he was giving a presentation for the company on a topic he knew quite well. At soon as he began, he completely froze and totally lost his place in his deck of flash cards. It was a disaster. We were concerned that the same mishap might occur during the Bloomberg interview because he would be talking to millions of listeners. But, given that there was no audience in his presence, and he had the ability to reference notes easily, he was confident that he would be able to pull it off. Right before it was time for him to begin, he panicked a bit and became extremely nervous. But, once he got going, he seemed to be fine. Once the interview was complete, he was relieved, excited and thought that he hit the interview out of the park.

About a week went by, and the producer from Bloomberg called us to schedule another interview. This time it was my turn, I did my prep work and the interview went as smoothly as the first. After the interview was complete, the moment that I had alluded to earlier occurred. The producer asked a question that changed the dynamic between my partner and me moving forward, from which we never recovered. She asked if I was available for the next interview. My director of business development came to me with the issue because he knew how much this would upset my partner. Remember, it was my partner's turn to do the next interview. In all fairness, it would have most likely upset me if the shoe was on the other foot. Knowing how much conflict this would cause, I asked my director to call the producer, explain the situation and make sure she knew that it was very important that we rotate the interviews.

Unfortunately, the producer of the show didn't like my partner's interview and wasn't interested in any future interviews with him. She explained that if our position was that it was both of us or none of us, then unfortunately the answer is none. They were, however, interested in continuing on with me and left the ball in my court. This was such a great opportunity for our firm and something we had been positioning ourselves for over many years. Finally, a large portion of the investment community would know how much we had to offer. It didn't make sense to forgo the opportunity. Therefore, the decision was made to have me do the next interview and not to tell my partner that they didn't want him. My director of business development started making excuses to my partner that there was some sort of miscommunication and that he would figure it out. At first, my partner was fine with it. Yet, after about ten interviews, it was clear that the tension brewing between us was growing.

Although, the tension continued to mount, some of this tension was overshadowed by the excitement of our employees. There was a tremendous amount of pride developing in the company that we were being interviewed on the radio and it materialized in the pace of our growth. After about thirty interviews on Bloomberg, it seemed as if my partner had settled in and the tension existing early on in the interview cycle was apparently waning. However, looks can be deceiving, because they were actually getting worse and exploded when the opportunity to be on television arose. Fox Business was a fledgling television network in 2008 and needed more talent to interview, which was my lucky break. Because I had experience on radio, it was enough for them to give me a chance on their network. Luckily, they liked me and continued to invite me back, which led to more coverage, more attention, more excitement and more pent up tension. Eventually, I was doing at least one interview per week, sometimes two or three.

While I was preparing for interviews, flying to New York to do live shots on Liz Claman's Countdown to the Closing Bell on Fox

Business, CNBC's Squawk Box, and even to get interviewed by ABC national nightly news the day that Steve Jobs stepped down from Apple because of his illness; my partner's ire towards me continued to fester. It eventually exploded when we were all working late one night, and my partner decided to start accusing me of stealing television away from him. He said that I was divisive and built my media success to his detriment. He claimed that I did it on purpose. He thought that it was all driven by my ego. Then, he revealed that he was going to go all in to fund a project that I had rejected because he was going to make it the most successful thing we had ever done. Basically, he announced that he had become my adversary.

We had been working with a fund manager for many years and we had a track record of massive success. But, it was a paper tiger. That is, all the fund ever did was track how much return would have been made, but there was no real data. When I ran all the numbers and accounted for market movement and trading fees, profit became unobtainable. Even though my partner didn't lift a finger in designing the fund, he was committed to its launch because he was convinced that it would be highly profitable for the company and didn't care that the best chance for the fund would be to break even. He went ahead with his project, completely against my better judgement. Unfortunately, he convinced half the company to market the fund to their clients, even though the analysis that was done regarding the performance of the fund pointed to its failure because of the high volume of trading and the internal fee structure. Even though I was completely opposed to the release of the fund, he convinced the other partner in the fund project to vote in favor of it, which made it a two-to-one vote. When I pressed my other partner to explain why he voted in favor of the release of the fund, even though he knew it was mathematically impossible for the clients to make any return on their investment, he said it's because he knew that my partner would throw a fit if he didn't get his way. It was definitely time for me to leave.

After the first two months of the fund launch it was already profitable, which led my partner to openly gloat at the company meetings and he made sure everyone knew that he was the mastermind behind the fund. However, the second month's peak ended up being the high watermark of the fund and it never achieved that level again.[34] Before I left the company that I helped found, the new fund was down almost fifty percent and our company was no longer what it once was. I went from having an ownership stake that was valued at $7.4 Million in 2008, to offloading my shares to my partners for ten cents on the dollar so that I could walk away. My decision to sell was made in mid-2012. Over the next six months, I sold all of my shares in the company and left to build a team from scratch at one of the largest Wealth Management firms in the industry. Coincidently, the sale of my company closed in March of 2013, the same month that the stock market had completely recovered.

When people asked me why I worked so hard all those years and left right when there was finally a light at the end of the tunnel my answer was quite simple. There came a point where I realized that I was in the wrong tunnel and the light at the end of it wasn't shining at me from the direction toward which I wanted to head. My goals for my clients and for myself were not going to be met with the partners I had and the platform that we were using. It was time for me to move on and I never looked back. The experience I went through gave me a clarity regarding who I was and who I wanted to become. I made the decision to take the risk of starting over, armed only with my faith that the new direction I was heading in was going to take me exactly where I wanted to go.

Through our greatest struggles come our most rewarding successes. Recovering from a global financial crisis was tough enough. Add to that an embezzling partner, a splintered corporate identity and a roadmap back to success filled with a bumpy trail of uncertainty. Bouncing back from leaving the company I helped build, along with the loss of millions of dollars that were earned over many years was the most difficult financial challenge I had faced up to that point in my life. However, I was armed with all the lessons I'd learned in my past and an understanding of how to build it back my way. That was the silver lining. Once you understand how to build a business from the ground up, as long as you have the emotional fortitude and resilience to do it, you can build up another business even better and even stronger.

"If you can't fly then run, if you can't run then walk,
if you can't walk then crawl, but whatever you do you
have to keep moving forward." - Martin Luther King Jr

CHAPTER 16

Always move forward

We often get stuck as we move toward our goals. We may reach a point at which we simply want to give up. We've identified our talents, have clarity in our vision, yet the obstacles that get in our way become too overwhelming to drive forward. This moment can occur even after our brains have been reprogrammed for a success mindset. This moment can occur even after we know that we are working towards the goals that are aligned with our talents. Perhaps you've even lost your faith and the sight of your ultimate goal. At these moments, moving forward is the best strategy. If you follow the success principle of streaking and micro-goals then none of these challenges should matter. If you are truly on a mission, you can find the strength to carry on because you are only focused on doing one simple micro-task, knowing that the accumulation of these tasks will eventually get you to your destination.

However, we are all human and sometimes life gets so overwhelming that we lose motivation, start questioning our goals and may even become depressed. At these times, it may be an advantage to think about other people who have faced monstrous challenges and overcame them. There are many examples of people who have struggled through tough times on the way to achieving their mission, but few like the story of Legson Kayira. He was a small boy, living in a small village but he had a huge vision. Raised in the mountains of Africa with little food and no education, Legson was a typical ten-year old boy in his part of the world. His achievements exemplify the principal of micro-goals, of always moving forward and are quite inspirational.

Legson learned how to read when a group of missionaries came to his remote village. As he was learning, his favorite book was one about the life of Abraham Lincoln, who overcame a poor upbringing, eventually attended college and became the 16th President of the United States of America. Lincoln's fortitude planted a seed of hope in Legson that he too could overcome his own obstacles, so he became obsessed with going to a university in the United States. He had no clue how he would do it, but with his mind set on a vision of a better life, he swore to himself that he would somehow achieve his goal.

When he was about sixteen years old, Legson told his parents that he was leaving to go to the United States. Then, without any support, he just started walking. There were three major challenges facing Legson during his journey: Africa is hot and barren for many stretches, it's difficult to communicate consistently because there are over 1,500 languages across the continent, and he had no money for his trip. He survived by sleeping in the streets, finding work doing odd jobs to afford food, and often was found to resort to begging when no jobs were to be found. Living like this for about fifteen months and having walked over 1,000 miles, Legson eventually ended up in Kampala, which is the capital of Uganda. Once there, he found a library, began researching American universities and settled on Skagit Valley College in Mount

Vernon Washington because the image of the University nestled in the clearing of a forest reminded him of the village in which he grew up.[35]

After receiving a letter from Legson describing his journey to Uganda and his goal to attend Skagit University, the admissions office replied to his correspondence. The registrars let him know that they were so impressed by his fortitude that if he could find a way to Skagit, they would give him a full scholarship. His heart was filled with joy as he realized that the only obstacle standing in his way of attending Skagit Valley College was a plane flight. However, after six-months of working odd jobs and saving every penny, Legson wasn't too much closer to being able to afford a plane ticket. Although he wasn't aware of this, his story had been spreading through the Skagit campus. A group of students had raised the sum of money Legson needed for a plane ticket to Washington. More than two years after he started his journey, Legson found himself on the doorstep of Skagit University with his two books, the clothes on his back, and his letter containing the promise of a scholarship.

Legson eventually graduated from Skagit, went on to earn a PhD, became a Political Science professor at Cambridge University in England, and grew to become a respected author and a beacon of light to anyone fortunate enough to learn the story of the little African boy who found his dream in a book and had enough courage to follow it. It's touching to hear about the triumph of a little boy who had a vision, overcame overwhelming odds in his quest to make that vision a reality, and created an amazing future for himself. Whenever you get stuck in a state of despair, remember that there is a Legson in all of us. We simply need to focus on moving forward each day to find him.

This may be an overwhelming task, unless you break your efforts down into micro-goals and take a step in the right direction each day. People like Legson Kayira somehow have this ability already. All high achievers do. Anyone can acquire this power by reprogramming their brains, fighting for their vision and keeping track of the streaks attached to their micro-goals. Even if you use this method, there will be times when you'll question your resolve. It might feel like the load you carry is too great, the end-goal you seek seems too far off, and the daily micro-goals aren't moving you any closer to your destination. Now especially, you must maintain faith that you will get there. No matter how difficult it feels, keep moving forward with the knowledge that you will eventually reach your desired goal. Although perseverance is easier said than done, it's a must.

If your struggle feels impossible, please think of sixteen-year-old Legson and how he overcome great odds to reach his goal. I'm not advising you to let his inspirational story be your strength, because as I've mentioned throughout this book, it can't. You are on the path to finding your own strength and have to rely on your own faith to get you through difficult times. However, whenever negative thoughts start creeping in as I face a challenge that seems overwhelming, I do think of Legson. I don't think about his journey, his challenges or even his triumphs. Instead, I ask myself one simple question, "Is what I'm going through right now easier or harder than walking through Africa for a year-and-a-half with no money, no clothes and no shelter?" To this point in my life, the answer has always been that it's been easier. This type of conversation with yourself will easily give you the ability to continue forward because you realize that nothing you do in life can ever be as difficult as walking across Africa. But, what do you do when you are losing faith in your personal mission? What if you continuously try your best, but it isn't good enough? You may be at a crossroads in your life and all the self-confidence in the world isn't going to help you reach your destination because you're stuck, as though you are knocking down a brick wall without the proper tools.

If you've done everything right but it becomes clear that you aren't likely going to reach the goal you set for yourself, you now need to take inventory of your strengths and weaknesses. Gary Vaynerchuk is one of the entrepreneurs and success coaches that speaks about this topic. Vaynerchuk is best known for his work in digital marketing and social media as the chairman of New York-based communications company, VaynerX.[36] In his discussions, he makes it abundantly clear that you shouldn't focus your energy on making your weaknesses your strengths. Instead, you should focus all your energy on making your strengths even stronger. Otherwise, you will end up striving for something you will never be great at, and only being good isn't what makes you successful. Too many people apply their massive sense of self-confidence and ability to achieve to some role for which they never will have talent, or in which they can never achieve excellence. The result is that they relegate themselves to a life of mediocrity because they are applying themselves to an activity at which they will never be proficient.

This observation brings us to the discussion of one of the most harmful motivational thoughts that, I believe, is spread throughout the motivational community. The idea is that you can have anything you want in life if you just believe in yourself. Anything? Really?

If you're not very coordinated, five-foot-six inches tall and have a vertical jump of less than ten inches then you will never be able to slam dunk a basketball. It doesn't matter how much belief you have, it will never happen for you, unless your arms happen to also be five feet long. The math on this one is not too difficult to figure out. Is this an extreme example? Not really. There are so many people that are searching to become someone that they can't be because their vision of what they want isn't in-line with their own gifts. It's not enough just to believe in yourself. You must also reach for something that you are capable of achieving. Otherwise, you will never be great but instead always will be in search of your true potential. The way to reach your true potential is to use a list of strengths you've inventoried and align them with a suitable goal.

This important concept bears repeating in a different way for maximum emphasis. The concept reminds us of the saying, "when the student is ready, the teacher will come." To achieve your true potential, you must believe in yourself AND you must reach for something that aligns with your natural talent. If you excel at math but can't sing very well, then reach for a goal that will involve math even if you want to be a singer. If you are an outstanding athlete but don't excel academically, then reach for a goal that will involve athletics even if you seek something academic. If you interact well with people but don't like coding computer algorithms, then reach for a goal that will involve working with others even if you want to be a coder. It's important to understand that sometimes what we want isn't aligned with our talents.

However, just because you can't excel in a field you really want to be part of, doesn't mean that you can't excel in another area that suits you even better. Ironically, you could ultimately achieve what you really want, but may take a different path to get there. Begin by asking yourself questions like, "Do I want to be a movie star, or do I want to be successful in the entertainment industry?" Those are two very different realities. You might not have a talent to act, but you may have a great vision of how to bring all the aspects of a movie together to produce a final product. So, why not apply your skills within the entertainment industry to become a director or a producer? I have a very good friend who did just that. He realized early in his career that he wanted to work behind the camera instead of in front of it and chose to become a producer. His decision was fueled by three key revelations. He accepted that he wasn't a great actor, but realized that he was very creative, and foresaw that his career would likely be a lot longer behind the camera than in front of it. You can produce movies for fifty years if you are outstanding at what you do. How many actors can anyone think of who have a fifty-year career? Very few. But many great producers have had careers that span that time frame. Perhaps you've noticed that during the Oscar presentations when all the grey-haired producers get invited to the stage to accept their awards.

My friend has achieved unexpected success because of the decision he made to live his Hollywood life making movies instead of starring in movies. One of the greatest aspects of his life is that he is anonymously famous, which is why I am not mentioning him by name. However, some of his best friends are famous actors who can't even go out in public without being cornered by rabid fans and even more rabid paparazzi. My friend has the benefit of hanging out with the stars and being part of the Hollywood scene. But he also has the benefit of being able to go out to dinner with his wife without being bothered. He enjoys the best of both worlds, results of his decision from which he's never looked back.

You may not want to be an actor, producer or rock star. Whatever path you are going to take, you need to figure out what you really want and if the vehicle to take you there aligns with your talent. Additionally, you will still need to work hard to cultivate that talent. Bruce Lee once said that it takes 10,000 repetitions to perfect a technique in martial arts.[37] Malcom Gladwell is often credited for the theory that it takes 10,000 hours to become an expert any field or skill.[38] Although the theory that repetition leads to ultimate success is now widely accepted and revered, imagine if Mark Zuckerberg worked 10,000 hours on his basketball skills. Chances are that you wouldn't have ever heard of him. Imagine if Kobe Bryant spent 10,000 hours coding in his basement. Chances are that you wouldn't have ever heard of him. The reason that Zuckerberg and Bryant reached the pinnacle of success in their respective fields is that their excruciatingly hard work was aligned with their gift. Believing in yourself and working hard are not sufficient. You need the combination of hard work and an understanding of your gift. Some people will never become champions because they simply chose the wrong sport.

The Billion Dollar question then becomes, how do you make sure that your career choice aligns with your talent? The answer isn't as complicated as you might think. First of all, you have to take a very honest inventory of your skillset. Luckily, life leaves you clues. One of the first clues that you have a particular talent is that you love working at it so much that it doesn't actually feel like work. Another clue is that, when you do it, other people consistently tell you that you make it look easy. A third clue is that you constantly think about it and are willing to risk everything to be the best at it. There are even more ways, beyond life's clues, to find your talent.

You can ask questions of yourself like, "What was I attracted to as a child?" Or, "What is the consistent theme that continuously runs through my mind?" The answer could be something simple like you were very attracted to fire and had a natural need of serving others. If these both continued to be strong themes in your life, then become a fireman/fireperson. If you aren't sure, or can't remember, ask friends and family members what they think you would be great at. Surprisingly, the people around you that love you will very often give you some insight that you weren't able to see yourself. Why? Very often it is difficult to see the entire picture when you are in it.

This concept of trying to see the whole picture of your life was first coined by the German psychologist, Fritz Perls. He named this concept Gestalt. The term Gestalt basically means that a configuration cannot be described simply as the sum of its parts. Perls realized that people become very myopic in their concept of themselves, as if they are staring at the painting of their own lives but are standing too close to see the whole thing. They remain focused on very small portions of the painting, establish their current focus on the most pressing need and tend to jump from need to need without stepping back and seeing the entire picture. This is why the opinions of others can help you in your quest to find yourself. Others see you with a different perspective and open the door to you seeing things about your life you never grasped before.

What is your strength? What can you talk about for hours and remain interested in? What types of books do you like to read? What subjects did you excel the most in when you were in school? These are useful questions to ask yourself when you are finding your talent. If financial success is important to you, it helps to focus on a talent that people will pay you to do. However you determine your talent, it is the key to expressing all you can be. Otherwise you run a risk of leading a life that is never fulfilled and one in which you never reach your unique and ultimate potential. Like Legson Kayira, you can walk through the dessert of Africa towards the goal that is right for you. Life will give you clues to guide you. Some people find their gift when they are five, and some find it when they are fifty-five. I can't tell you when you'll find yours. However, I urge you to start looking.

"It's a funny thing about life, once you begin to take note of the things you are grateful for, you begin to lose sight of the things that you lack." - Germany Kent

CHAPTER 17

Wake up early and be grateful

Here's a secret that you need to know. Almost no one likes waking up. Why did I say "almost" and not "no one?" Well, there are exceptions. Our circadian rhythm is an internal process that regulates our sleep-wake cycle.[39] Some early risers are those rare individuals who have been blessed with a circadian rhythm that has made them morning people. The rest are those who have programmed themselves to begin each day with a burst of energy. For those who don't have that natural circadian gift, how do they get this energy? They must rely on the excitement of being alive and the chance to face the day ahead because they have formed the habit of doing so.

Years ago I read that most CEOs of Fortune 500 companies wake up four hours before they get to the office and tackle the most important tasks of the day first. The most recent article I found supporting this assertion was written by Marie Johnson for ladders.com. Johnson says that an early wake-up call is one of the most universal habits among today's CEOs. Then she lists specific examples of New Jersey

Nets CEO Brett Yormark who gets up at 3:30 a.m., Virgin America CEO David Cush who starts his day at 4:15 a.m., and Disney CEO Bob Iger who says he gets up at 4:30 a.m. every morning. The list of early risers continues and includes names like Apple CEO Tim Cook, Square CEO Jack Dorsey, and Xerox CEO Ursula Burns. Regardless of the specific CEO or specific company named, the idea behind the principle remains the same: If you want to join the ranks of today's top CEOs, you won't do so by staying in bed.[40]

Why should you convince yourself to join the ranks of the successful and sacrifice your sleep to do so? If you want to be among the ranks of the successful, then you shouldn't need convincing. There is one trick you can use that can help you understand that you may already have the ability to wake up early every day within you, but you may not know it. Think about a time that you woke up to go on a trip that you had been planning for six months. Didn't you wake up excited and ready to go? In fact, didn't you wake up before your alarm went off because you simply couldn't wait to get dressed and get out the door? If you have this attitude before a vacation, or maybe some other special pending event in your life, why can't you be that enthusiastic every morning? Some say that if your dream is big enough and your plan for the day is exciting enough that you can get yourself into this state on a daily basis. You will then become one of the lucky few who make this ritual of waking up early a daily habit.

Although you should strive to be "I'm going to Disneyland" excited every single morning, I don't think it's something you can rely on. Most mornings you will wake up and the first thought you have is not one of excitement, but of hitting the snooze button and staying in your warm bed. What then? You need to understand that another important characteristic that successful people possess is that they do things in spite of not wanting to do them. You might never want to wake up early on any day for the rest of your life, and that's okay, as long as you overcome the voice that tells you to snooze for just another ten minutes and get up anyway. If you can't bring yourself to do it, then there is an easy way to make it happen. Have you guessed what that is? Of course you have. The answer is that you would start a streak.

From now on, every day when your alarm goes off, jump right out of bed immediately then vocalize how grateful you are to be alive. This is a very important step because starting the day off with gratitude sets your mood for the day. Whether it's the simple vocalization of gratitude, thanking God for the day as I do, or your own personal ritual of gratitude, waking up early and being grateful every day can do wonders for your self-confidence and level of joy. Then, remember to record in your streak journal that you got up early and were grateful for the day. This could be one of the most important streaks you start. If you are grateful for what you have now, no matter what the present condition of your life, you open yourself up to receiving whatever it is that you are working towards. On the other hand, if you aren't grateful for what you have today, why would that change in the future? Because today is yesterday's tomorrow, you must remain grateful every day. One of these days your future will be your past. To attract what you want, you have to want what you have. There aren't too many concepts that are more important than this.

To illustrate this point, think of someone who complains every time they receive a gift. Whenever you purchase a gift for them, they either complain or are clearly disappointed. Then, they either do not use the gift you gave them, or they return it. If this occurs once in a while, this would be acceptable. However, imagine if this was consistent behavior. Eventually the effect would be that you would be programmed to assume that there could be no gift you can give that would make them happy. This is called learned helplessness and can be devastating to the dynamics of a relationship.[41] You might eventually stop giving them gifts completely, or at the very least, you wouldn't invest a lot of energy or thought into the gifts because your gifts will never be appreciated anyway.

On the other hand, imagine if the person you gave the gift to was thrilled and full of gratitude. When they open your gift with wide eyes, a big smile and show genuine gratitude for the gift then you would be filled with joy as well. Their display of gratitude would be contagious. What if, beyond the gratitude they express, you see the gift you have given them displayed in their home or office? Or, if the gift was an article of clothing, what if you see it in pictures they might post on their social media? You would feel appreciated and want to give them more gifts in the future. Such is human nature.

Your subconscious resembles the ungrateful recipient of your gift in the example of gift giving. When life gives you a gift, no matter how big or how small, if you aren't grateful consistently then life will eventually stop delivering you gifts. However, if you are grateful, then life will want to keep granting you gifts. Make it a priority to remember that every day you have something to be grateful for, regardless of the difficulties you may be facing. You must force yourself to get up every morning, thank God for the day, and be grateful for all that you have. Will it always be easy? Nope! Sometimes your life might be so filled with struggles that you may only be grateful that you have a set of legs that allow you to get up out of bed. If that's where you are, then that's where you are. Be grateful for your legs, your feet and the shoes you put on your feet. That's a start.

As was touched upon in Chapter 15, I learned this lesson first-hand when life hit me in the face like a ton of bricks at the end of 2008. I had finally reached the point in my life that all my previous challenges had been overcome. Challenges of an impoverished youth.

Challenges of overcoming bullying and abuse. Challenges of grinding away through the University, Graduate School, and then a career in which I worked fourteen-hour days for five years until I finally was able to buy into my own company. I lived in a multi-million home, was making over one million dollars a year, had a beautiful wife, a beautiful daughter and a great dog. After over a decade of grinding it out, I was 38 years old and living the dream. Then, all of a sudden, the financial crisis of 2008 came out of nowhere. All of a sudden, everything in my life turned upside down and I was faced with a choice. Was I going to succumb to the pressure, cave and fall apart? Or, was I going to get up every morning, find something to be grateful about, and get to work? I chose the latter.

As difficult as it was, I became rooted in thinking only about the positives in my life. Having health is always better than having wealth, although having both is better. Additionally, having the knowledge of how to make money is always better than having money without the knowledge because if you lose your money, you can always earn more. Having love in your life is better than being alone. So, each day I woke up with gratitude that I had my health, that I was knowledgeable in my field and that I had a loving wife and daughter. Not only were those blessings on my list, but I began to appreciate basic gifts like my two hands, my two feet, and my two eyes. Going through the financial crisis made me take inventory of all the many advantages in my life and I was truly grateful for them. This attitude gave me the strength to eventually transition to my new company, rebuild my income, and to honor the experience.

The transition was difficult, as most transitions are. As the proverb states, "when God closes one door, another opens up." But, the proverb doesn't mention that the walk through the hallway from the closed door to the open door may be hell. It only took me five years to get back to where I needed to be. Those five years sometimes felt like an eternal sentence in purgatory. It's strange how time works in our lives. When we are doing something that's fun and exciting, time goes by so quickly. When we are doing something difficult, challenging and maybe even painful, time goes by so slowly. Yet, when it's over and you are looking back, both spans of time are only memories. Armed with the knowledge of how time works, or knowing that there was a light at the end of the tunnel, or even knowing that I was working for the security of my family didn't help time go by any faster. Knowledge of these things did, however, help my focus and my resolve to continue being grateful every single day, regardless of the challenges that had to be overcome. It also gave me the confidence to make the decision to sell my shares in the company that I'd just worked so hard to help rebuild because there wasn't a fear associated with the process. If you follow the process, are grateful to be alive and forge ahead toward your goals, you can live your life with confidence.

When my wife asked me if I was sure that I was making the right decision to sell, especially after the difficult journey we had just endured together, the answer was an easy "yes" and the explanation as to why was quite simple. I explained to my wife that my goal was to elevate my business to a new and higher level of service, and to provide better resources and execution to my clients. However, if I stayed with my current company then we would end up stuck exactly where we were at that moment. While I was giving her this explanation, I was drawing an imaginary line between where we were and where we were ultimately headed. She immediately understood that the further I travelled down the wrong road, then the further I would move away from the ultimate destination. She supported my decision, which made it a lot easier to stay on course.

Without going into the additional details of my next building phase, which took another five years, the important point for you to understand is that I made the decision to focus on what I was walking towards and not on where I had been. Once the decision had been made to move forward, the principles that had been used to rebuild my old company were applied to building my new business. Moving forward consisted of completing daily activities specifically designed for progress towards my goal, as well as keeping myself accountable for the execution of these daily activities. Just like I did, anyone who is armed with the knowledge of the tasks they need to complete on any given day and who has developed the ability to follow through on those tasks can reach their desired destination. What's needed is discipline, hard work and focus. Having a positive attitude and a sense of joy while you are grinding through your personal hell doesn't hurt either. So, wake up every single morning with a smile on your face and with a sense of gratitude. Then, take a deep breath and commit to marching forward that day like a champion. If you string enough of these days together, you will reach your destination, regardless of where you are now.

*"Courage is being scared to death and
saddling up anyway." - John Wayne*

CHAPTER 18

You must have the courage
to face your fears

When I walked away from my company and started out to rebuild my business from scratch, even though I felt great fear every step of the way, my decision to move forward had already been made. Without committed decisions, most progress by the human race would cease. Remember, it's decision that dictates action and not the fear of the action. Also remember that you would have to be a sociopath if life-altering decisions weren't accompanied by fear.

You've most likely heard the phrase, "fear isn't real." That statement simply is not true. Fear is very real. When you are sitting at the edge of an airplane doorway ready to jump out, with your heart pounding in your chest and one breath away from a panic attack, that fear is more real than most emotions you will experience. That visceral sensation is your biology kicking in to protect you from harm. However, your rational human system allows you to override that biological system and gives you a choice. You can succumb to your fear and crawl back into the plane or separate yourself from your fear and take a leap of faith.

This ability is one of the traits that separates humans from animals. Although animals are very much like us, even feeling love and attachment, it is quite doubtful that they have the ability to understand the world on a conceptual level because this level of thought requires language.[42] For example, wolves live in packs because instinct drives them to do so. However, they don't understand the concept of community. They don't understand that they live in a homogenous group with shared values and that pack life will aid in their safety and lead to a continued propagation of their species. They don't understand the concepts of democracy, philosophy or religion. Humans have been given the gift of being able to understand concepts, which allows them to over-ride their biological programming.

Even greater than conceptualization, humans have been given the ability to explain these concepts through language. Language may be the most important tool that humans have developed because it is the cornerstone of all our other abilities. When you study the history of language, you will note that it developed so humans could share pictures. We use words to describe the picture we have in our mind. Someone hears those words, interprets them and then the picture that forms in the receiver's mind is the same as the picture that was formed in the mind of the communicator. The better we are at explaining when we are the communicator, and the better we are at understanding when we are in receipt of the communication, the more successful we become in our society. Language gives us the ability to, not only explain what we are thinking, but to learn how to think differently if we want to change our environment. This is such a phenomenal gift and allows us to grow in ways that animals can't even imagine. Think about it. A dog can only ever be a dog, a lion can only ever be a lion, but you can be someone other than you are today because you can make different choices. You can choose to be a different person!

What's most important to understand about your ability to make a choice in the face of fear, is that the outcome that you are fearing probably isn't real. When you are sitting at the edge of an opening in a plane and getting ready to jump out with a parachute strapped to your back, you have the ability to embrace the fear of that moment and do it anyway. You can do this, not because fear doesn't exist, but because you are willing to move forward even though you understand that the outcome may be one you don't like. When you ask someone out on a date, you face rejection. When you ask for a raise from your boss, you face dejection. When you tell people about your dreams, you face ridicule. So what! Many people walking around today, and you may be one of them, are deathly afraid of one or all of the aforementioned situations. Here's something you need to hear. You must change your fear mindset if you are to exceed your own expectations and reach the level of success you desire.

It's great if your dream is so crystal clear and motivating that you can wake up every day, ready to go with a smile on your face. But, if you're relying only on that feeling, you will ultimately fail. If you only rely on your feelings to make positive decisions, you won't take action most of the time because we usually avoid anything that is challenging, uncomfortable or painful. Remember, there are two distinct voices that battle for our attention every day. There is that voice telling you that you are great the way you are and you don't need to strive to be anyone else, so just sit on the couch and watch TV. After all, you deserve it. Or, even worse, it's that voice telling you that you aren't good enough and you will most likely fail at whatever it is you are striving for, so you might as well give up.

Fortunately, you have another voice. For some, it's just a whisper. But faint as it is, it's present. Perhaps it's the small voice you had as a child telling you that you have the ability to venture forward and live your dream. Remember what that voice was like when you had your whole life ahead of you? It's the voice that told you that you were going to be an astronaut, a fireman, or a ballerina. If that voice is so faint inside you, you must ask yourself, "why did I let the voice almost die?" That's an important question you have to ask yourself because only you can bring back this voice. Only you can resurrect it. Once you do, you will give this voice the strength to grow from a slight whisper into a bellowing scream and drown out the voice of doubt that may be holding you back.

But how? It's by having an understanding that the conflicting voices in your head are all starving for your attention and the one you pay the most attention to is the one that grows strong. Therefore, all you have to do is feed the positive voice and starve the other ones. You must feed the voice telling you that you are great, that you deserve the best, that you deserve to reach your goals. You must feed the voice telling you that you still have a great life to live, that today your life is just beginning, that you are starting your journey. If you feed that voice, then the other ones will slowly wither away and become a mute memory. If you don't learn to do this, then the battle that rages inside you between saying "yes" to taking the action you need to in order to move forward toward your goals and saying "no" to that action will rage on. Stop the battle that is waging war inside your head and learn to focus only on the voice that allows you to forge ahead towards your wishes, hopes and desires.

Has this advice been given by many people over the decades? Yes, it has. Like all other advice you've heard about success, it sounds great because it is great. However, it takes someone truly special to follow through with the advice because it's so difficult to increase the volume of your positive self-talk to a level that will drown out the negative. To develop the habit of positive self-talk, you need to design micro-goals that will allow you to conquer that negative voice. I'm going to warn you right now that this is one of the hardest things you will have to do, but the rewards for doing it are ultimate success, fulfillment and happiness.

To help you understand exactly what you're up against, you need to meet the Keeper of the Gate. The concept of the Keeper is one of the most influential that I have ever learned. It's been passed down for generations, possibly originating from the teachings of ancient Japanese Martial Arts. Luckily, a friend of mine passed it on to me. My friend, Robert, was an all-state high school wrestler prior to his service to our country in the military, and I had the honor of training with him in full-contact martial arts while I was in college. Wrestlers are a different breed because they only have one speed, which is full speed and they only have one direction, which is forward. He was my biggest challenge, became my best training partner, and we are still friends to this day.

Years after we stopped training together, we were having a conversation in front of my house as he was heading home after a visit. I was always impressed with his work ethic and asked him where it came from. He told me that it came from many different influences in his life. But, the main three were his years of wrestling, his time in the military and a story he was told when he was young about the Keeper of the Gate. Curious, I asked him to explain. He explained it to me as his grandfather had originally explained it to him.

Each one of us has the knowledge of the entire Universe locked away in our brains. It was implanted there by God and it's ours to access when we are ready. However, if we aren't ready for the information and we receive it too soon, we won't be able to handle it. It would be like sending an infant to hunt a lion. Therefore, we must train our minds to such a level that we can digest the information, and also know what to do with it once we receive it. Because this information is so valuable, it's heavily guarded by the Keeper of the Gate, whose sole purpose in life is to make sure that we never get to the information. This is done in order to protect us from receiving the information too soon. The Keeper is more intelligent than we are and knows what we are thinking. Therefore, it's almost impossible to overcome the Keeper to unlock the knowledge of the Universe. Herein is the catch. The only way we can grow worthy to receive the knowledge of the Universe is to overcome the Keeper. However, every time we get smart enough to beat the Keeper, the Keeper also grows smarter and finds a way to beat us. It becomes a never-ending loop.

So, how do we beat the Keeper? Surprisingly, it's not in the big things we do in our life, but in the little things. Beating the Keeper is a slow act of attrition and takes many years. It's in the little things that we are beaten, and we must learn to win at these little things to prevail and claim our prize.

For example, when you come home, see dishes in the sink and think, "I'll sit down and relax. I can do those later." Congratulations, you just lost and are further away from beating the Keeper because laziness won. When you get ready for bed and toss your clothes on the floor instead of placing them in the hamper, it's another loss. When you pick up the phone to make that call that you know you have to make and then set the phone down in order to do something that may be easier, you lose again. It's in those little things we do every single day about which we hesitate and decide not to do that we continuously lose. The only way to overcome these tendencies that allow the Keeper to keep winning is with the acknowledgement of the Keeper's existence. Once you are conscious that the Keeper is there, your whole life changes. Suddenly, overcoming your own bad habits and ignoring the voice that tells you to be lazy, complacent or irresponsible becomes a bit of a game.

The next time you need to do something and procrastinate, even for a moment, say to the Keeper, "You're not beating me today" and then do what you were supposed to do. Then, take pride that you just came a step closer to winning the ultimate prize of all the knowledge of the Universe. Soon, it becomes a game that you are playing all day and every day and your productivity increases to a level you can't imagine because the voice that drives you is no longer the good voice or the bad voice, but your own voice! The Keeper really isn't anything but another representation of the lazy part of your sub-conscious. However, human beings are much better at dealing with concepts that have a face or a name. By giving that part of your consciousness that is trying to hold you back a name and by looking at the entire process of beating the Keeper as a game that you must win, you set yourself up for ultimate success.

This may seem like a difficult concept to understand because we all tend to have a very loose definition of the brain and of the mind, and often use these words interchangeably. To really understand how to take control of your life, you need to understand the difference between the two. Your brain is the physical membrane of grey matter that sits between your ears and fires electrical signals through the synaptic channels giving you the ability to think and control bodily functions.[43] In contrast, the mind is synonymous with thought. Namely, the private conversation we have with ourselves that we carry on "inside our head."[44] If you can't wrap your thoughts around this concept, you're not alone. This is a conversation that is beyond religion, philosophy or science.

The mind has been called the self, the subconscious, the spirit, the soul, and has many other descriptions. It is much like the concept of gravity. It's a force that we can't see and can't touch, but we know it's there. We think we understand it when we apply the laws of physics, but that understanding is only conceptual. Sometimes in life, it's easier not to ask too many questions. Your mind is the amazing part of you that can drive you to the goals and aspirations you seek, so accept the gift you have been given. Take the gift, saddle up and ride.

Although the concept of the mind is elusive, successful people have learned how to use it and apply the definition of the mind within its most utilitarian function. It's a bit simpler if you start to think of everything physical about you as a tool, where the mind is the writer of the music and the brain is conductor of the band. If you wish to get up out of your chair and walk, your brain sends a signal to all the parts of the body that will be needed for this endeavor. It's the same for all your activities. But what tells the brain to send those signals? It's the mind. The mind is ultimately in control because it tells your brain what to do, even to think. Although your brain does the physical thinking through the firing of its synapses and sends those signals to the parts of the body that need to function for whatever task is at hand, all that thought is just a complex code that gets uploaded to the mind. The mind needed the brain to be the processor of the action of thought, but the mind will use that thought for its benefit. Label it as you must, but it's the mind that is in control of everything. The strong mind knows that it is the only voice you need, and it controls the voices inside your brain, including the voice of the Keeper.

Why are we even labeling some voice in our head as the Keeper in the first place? It's because the definition of mind has been elusive and difficult to understand. Each of us deals with voices in our heads that we typically define as the subconscious. Since this Japanese parable is so old, it's based upon an ancient attempt to explain how we deal with our mind and how we deal with the voices that live inside our heads. We still can use the same parable today, even with all our advanced understanding of neurobiology. Although we have a much better understanding of how the brain works than the ancient Japanese culture did, it seems quite clear that they understood the concept of mind and how to use it in pragmatic ways.

The mind is our essence and should be what controls the brain, the body and our emotions. However, as the mind attempts to maintain this control, there is a nagging voice telling us to be lazy, to avoid working out, or to order that dessert that we know we shouldn't eat. That negative voice will continue on and, unless you defeat it, the knowledge of how to become the ultimate version of yourself will continue to be locked away. When you overpower that voice and do that "thing" it was trying to talk you out of doing, you chip away at the voice's power. Labeling this voice as the Keeper gives it an identity. You will no longer be fighting against an elusive concept. Instead, you will have an enemy that has a name.

To defeat the voice of negative self-talk and to ensure that positive self-talk is the only voice you hear, your micro-goal must become to see how many days in a row you can beat the Keeper of the Gate. You may be thinking that this is too simplistic a goal. But it really isn't. If you attach these victories to a streak, then you get a little surge of dopamine, which gives you the incentive to continue beating this voice. In addition, this consistent action will slowly rewire your brain and strengthen it as a tool that is more aligned with your mission. Eventually, your mind will be doing all the talking and will have direct control over your brain, muting any other voices. Then, you will have finally beaten the Keeper, made your mind one with your thought and unlocked the true secret to success and belief in yourself.

You will then be in the state of flow. There will be no past and no future and only the present will exist. You will live in a pure state of "doing," with an instantaneous response to whatever your mind orders the brain to do. There will be no hesitation because you are now wired for success. This incredible transformation will give you the ultimate power and control over your thoughts and actions. Think of this as the difference between an electric car and a gas combustion engine. When you step on the accelerator of an electric car, you have instant torque. There is no delay in the acceleration. However, no matter how well a combustion engine is built, there is always a slight delay in acceleration because the torque is not instantaneously accessible. Imagine if you could have instant torque in your life whenever you face a new challenge. When you beat the Keeper, this acceleration can be yours.

"Where there is no vision, there is no hope" - George Washington Carver

CHAPTER 19

Visualize success

From the teachings of Zig Ziglar, to what's written in Rhonda Byrn's, *The Secret* and in so many other materials on success, the power of visualization is a consistent theme. It's taught in many different ways and by using many different methods. Although the exact formula regarding how to use visualization isn't the same from source to source, one thing is abundantly clear: You must visualize your success so that you understand where you are heading and so that you give yourself the best chance of getting there. Visualization is important for success for three key reasons. Visualizing what you want creates a target in your mind that you can see clearly and work toward. Secondly, visualization provides a laser focus on the goals you are moving towards. Finally, the practice subconsciously drives your attention toward people and situations that can help you in your efforts. All three reasons reinforce the possibility that you will reach your goals.

In May of 1961, President John F. Kennedy set a goal for our country reach the Moon.[45] At the time, we didn't have the technology to do it. But JFK realized that we were falling behind the Soviet Union in the space race, which had grown into a political issue. He understood how important it was to beat the Soviets and reach the moon so that the United States would remain as the dominant global power. When President Kennedy set the goal to reach the moon, it was a dream that most assumed would never come true and JFK may have overreached when he set the goal. Although his goal seemed far-fetched at the time, what was the effect upon the citizens of the United States? The goal launched the U.S. on a course to an uncharted destination that became backed by a national consciousness. It was a collective visualization that focused the nation on one result. When such single mindedness is achieved, it's difficult to stand in the way.

JFK inspired everyone to believe that we could send a rocket, with a velocity so great that it could carry three grown men out of our atmosphere, safely land it 240,000 miles away by using a trajectory that had not yet been found and return it safely back to the Earth. At the time, conventional wisdom was that this journey would be impossible to achieve. But the country rallied around this vision because the Soviet Union posed an existential threat as a growing world power. The country accepted a united assumption that the United States would not let the Soviets win the space race. Whether you agree with such a nationalistic spirit or not, it's clear that JFK found a way to incorporate the spirit of competition against, what was then considered to be, a mortal enemy. The vision of victoriously conquering the Soviets by reaching the moon first was inspiring. Although Kennedy initiated the project, it wasn't complete until years after his death. But, in July of 1969, the United States landed three men on the moon and changed the world's definition of human limitations.

The lesson we can take from this example is twofold. First, a goal must be worthwhile to inspire visualization. That is, it should be tied to a bold vision larger than yourself. Second, when visualizing a goal, you must paint a picture of the ultimate endpoint, which will create the focus you need to get there. Even if you've gone through these two steps, visualization often fails because of the lack of short-term reward available for our long-term goals. As previously discussed, nature has played a trick on us with the way our incentive-reward system has been designed. We are rewarded for the small actions we take from day-to-day. However, the reward we receive for achieving a long-term goal is not commensurate with the effort it took to achieve that goal. We can visualize all we like, but unless we are truly committed to the work it takes to achieve that vision, we can't ever accomplish it.

Thomas Edison said that, "a dream without action is simply a hallucination." Therefore, between visualization and success is work. Books like, *The Secret* by Rhonda Byrn can be useful when it comes to learning how to focus on your dream.[46] When you visualize your target clearly and concentrate on it consistently, you will more easily recognize the circumstances that can lead you to that outcome. This is not a new concept. In his landmark book on the subject, *Think and Grow Rich* that was originally published in 1937, Napoleon Hill wrote that you must create a clear mental picture of who you want to become in order to eventually actualize that picture.[47] But, visualization was never meant to be a substitute for work. On the contrary, it was intended as the first step in striving for success. The next step is planning, and the last step is executing. Which step is the most important? I would argue that it's the last step. Simply because results come as a reward for action.

Many people assert the value of designing a "dream board" filled with pictures of everything they want in life. They claim that by focusing on the outcomes pictured on their board, the universe will miraculously deliver them. I would counter to those people that there's an important portion of that claim that's missing. If you visualize getting checks in the mail and that is all you do, then what you will get in the mail are cancelations and eviction notices. You must take action for your dreams to come true because dreams without action are just dreams. It's still important to write down your goals and visualize them so that you know what you are striving for. With a clear image in your mind of your goals, positive developments will come your way and will help you in your journey. However, you will need to act on these blessings that materialize.

We'll use the example of the actor Jim Carey, who credits his success in the entertainment industry to his visualization techniques. When he was still a poor and out-of-work actor in the early 1990's, he wrote a check to himself from Hollywood for ten-million dollars for acting services rendered. The check was post-dated and payable in full in 1995. From that moment, he would drive up to the top of the Hollywood Hills in his beat-up car and visualize his ten-million-dollar paycheck while staring at this tattered check that he carried with him constantly in his wallet. Miraculously, he signed a contract in 1995 to play the lead role in the movie "Dumb and Dumber," which gave him a ten-million-dollar guarantee.[48] Amazingly, he landed that contract during the same exact year for which he had written the fictitious check to himself all those years before. Although visualizing the check was paramount to his success, it only played a part in the story. The actual work required to achieve that result wasn't discussed in his story of visualization, suggesting that all he did for ten years was to visualize that check.

What Jim doesn't talk about in his story of visualization is his relentless effort through many arduous years of struggle that eventually lead to his roles in television and the movies. What Jim doesn't talk about are countless hours he spent as a child entertaining his mother, who was addicted to pain medication, by learning how to be a master of physical comedy because it always made her laugh.[49]

Nor does he mention the years he spent writing comedic material for himself and for characters he developed before he landed a role in the show *In Living Color*.[50] He also leaves out that he spent thousands of hours working comedy clubs at night and going to auditions during the day before he landed his first movie role. So many years of work filled the time between the day he wrote the check to himself and the day he received it from Hollywood. The visualization gave him a sort of certainty that he was moving towards something, attracted events and people into his life that helped him throughout his journey, and allowed him to define his worth. These factors all helped him as he made progress toward the target he had set for himself. But, the biggest factor was that Jim Carey did the all the work.

There are countless of other examples of highly successful individuals who had a vision, crafted a plan to reach that vision, and executed on their plan through hard work. From athletes, to actors, to Nobel-Prize-Winning economists, not one ever reached a high level of success by only sitting on their couch and visualizing it. Unless they were "trust fund babies" or won the lottery, their success came from working toward a vision and staying firm with their convictions. It's important that you first write down your goals so that you know what the big picture is. Then, it's important that you break down those goals into micro-goals so that you can get that sense of accomplishment as you slowly chip away at achieving them. Even though you only focus your action on the micro-goals, you still should continue to visualize the end result you are targeting. By doing this, you will know where you are heading and will also be driven to take the action needed for you to get there.

"Life is suffering." - Buddha

CHAPTER 20

To succeed in life, you must suffer

Quotes often get misinterpreted, especially when they are taken out of context or inappropriately applied. For many, Buddha's statement that life is suffering has become a phrase of acceptance, almost to the extent that people allow themselves to become victims of life. The Buddha's message may imply that we should roll over in the face of pain and suffering and take it on the chin. However, if interpreted constructively, this quote offers some amazing insight and is very similar to a comment that has been made by ex-Navy SEAL and extreme athlete, David Goggins, who says that, "to be successful in life, you must suffer."[51] Although it's not exactly the same quote, there is a logical connection between the Buddha and Goggins' theories.

Buddha's quote said nothing about success and was just a blanket statement that life is suffering. The essence of Goggins' quote is that success is the outcome of suffering. Therefore, life is the outcome of suffering. That is, in order to truly live, we must be willing to suffer. In fact, it's what makes us human. It's through suffering that we overcome adversity. It's through suffering that we get a greater appreciation of life's moments of comfort. It's through suffering that we find our self-worth. The journey we take towards our ultimate success is forged by our ability to suffer. The more we can endure that suffering, the more successful we become. The message is that, through suffering, we can ultimately achieve the best version of ourselves.

Consider the story of the butterfly and the cocoon, which comes from an unknown origin and has many variations. However, the lesson is the same in each version, which is that we need to struggle in order to be at our best.

A man found the cocoon of a butterfly and brought it home with him. One day, a small opening appeared in the cocoon. He sat and watched the cocoon for several hours as the butterfly struggled to force its body through the little hole. Then, it seemed to stop making progress. It appeared as if the butterfly had progressed as far as it could and could go no further. The man decided to help the butterfly in its struggle. He took a pair of scissors and snipped off the remaining bit of the cocoon and the butterfly emerged easily. As the butterfly emerged, the man was surprised. It had a swollen body and small, shriveled wings. He continued to watch the butterfly expecting that, at any moment, the wings would dry out, enlarge, expand and eventually support the swollen body. He was hopeful that, in time, the body would contract, the wings would grow and the butterfly would be able to fly. However, that didn't happen. In fact, the butterfly spent the rest of its life crawling around with a swollen body and shriveled wings and was never able to fly.

In his kindness and haste, the man did not understand that the restrictive nature of the cocoon and the struggle of the butterfly to fight its way to freedom from this cocoon were required for the butterfly to achieve flight. The butterfly must be allowed to push its way through the tiny opening to force the fluid to leave its body. Additionally, the struggle of the butterfly to force its wings to break out of the cocoon's encasing builds the strength necessary to flap its wings. Only by struggling can the butterfly's body and wings both be ready for flight once it emerges from the cocoon.

Sometimes struggles are exactly what we need in our life. If God allowed us to go through life without any obstacles, it would cripple us. We would not grow as strong as we could have and we would never be able to fly.

We hear words of wisdom from the likes of Buddha, Goggins and from within the story of a butterfly. Yet, we rarely apply these lessons in our lives. Overprotective parents are often seen shielding their children from pain, injury or hardship. These parents want to spare their children from having to go through what they did when they were growing up and can't bear to see their own children suffering. However, like with the butterfly, overprotective parents create weak children. These parents don't realize that the pain children go through to overcome their challenges is exactly what they need to develop the grit that parents want so much for their kids.

How often do you see a great person come from a great person? This situation is rare. Most self-made millionaires go bankrupt two or three times before they finally create sustained wealth. Yet, they forget that the struggle is what made them who they are and don't want their kids to go through a similar struggle. They forget that the character of success they've built will not occur in their children unless they suffer as well. Many people never become the best version of themselves because they haven't experienced enough pain and suffering in their lives. The only way to develop the character it takes to excel in life is to learn how to get through the suffering and emerge on the other side.

You develop character while overcoming challenges that help transform you into a better version of yourself. Perhaps you have observed this in your own life. Have you ever bumped into a friend that you haven't seen in a while and you tell each other you how much each of you has changed? You may not have noticed changes in yourself because you live with yourself every day. But your friend hasn't seen you grow over time, nor have you seen them do the same. So, they notice the changes in you, and you notice the changes in them. Change is how we measure growth. To reach higher goals, you need to become a different person because the current version of you can't climb that high.

Often fear of change is an obstacle to moving forward and you get stuck. Fear anchors you to the current version of yourself and stunts your ability to grow if you can't overcome it. To have the life you've never possessed, you have to become someone that you've never been. But, how can anyone do this?

Each time we overcome a challenge and reach a new level of mastery, we become a better version of our previous self and now have the ability to take on greater challenges. Once we reach the highest peak we can see, we can then have the ability to see another. Our journey towards excellence is a constant struggle to reach each new peak. It's in the struggle that we achieve our success. This is why people like David Goggins put themselves into situations that involve suffering. If you are one of the people who tend to avoid the suffering that comes with the challenges you face, then your wings will never grow strong enough to support you. Eventually, you will be grounded for life. However, if you can become comfortable with being uncomfortable and learn how to keep fighting while facing adversity, then you can continue to grow, continue to achieve greater success and continue to rewire your brain to reach even higher levels of success. You can then define who you are as a person and take control of the direction of your life, of your happiness and of your ultimate destination.

"The most interesting lessons often lie in the mundane – those aspects of everyday life that locals take for granted and tourists tend to overlook." - Esther Dyson

Find joy in mundane tasks

I love washing the dishes! Seriously. Also, it's not in the, "I'm so positive in everything that I do in life" way that makes everyone around you want punch you in the face or question your sincerity. Such is the annoying positivity of the barista at your local coffee shop who has sipped too many espressos by 6:00am that their caffeine induced joy makes you ill. I experience a true sense of happiness washing dishes because the activity gives me a chance to meditate, pray and visualize the future. Sometimes the greatest revelations can come when you are soaping up a pan that you are getting ready to scrub like your life depended on it. Sometimes the greatest conversations with God occur when you are rinsing off plates before placing them into the dishwasher. Often, the best daydreams of your future self will come when you are in the middle of drying off the dishes that can't go into the dishwasher with a kitchen towel before you put them away.

A twofold connection occurs when one performs the task of washing dishes. First, we are naturally connected to water, which has a soothing effect while we are touching it for extended periods of time.[52] Second, we tend to "zone out" when we are completing routine tasks that don't require a lot of brain power and we become more connected to ourselves. When you put the two together, you can achieve the ability to find joy in the simple task at hand. Additionally, you feel satisfied when you are done. If you want to link this situation to our incentive-reward system, we get a reward that is commensurate with the task at hand because a pile of dishes can be washed in less than thirty minutes. Therefore, the surge of dopamine we receive as we complete this simple chore provides us a high level of value.

Why, then, do so many people hate doing dishes? My theory is that the perspective they take in the dishwashing task is one of negativity, rather than one of positive expectation. We've already discussed that your joy in life largely depends on your perspective and that this perspective is linked to the dopamine rush associated with it. How does that apply to mundane tasks like washing dishes? When you are washing the dishes, you are operating in two planes of consciousness. One plane is within the focus you are using to complete the task at hand, and the other is within the subconscious daydreaming that takes place in between the conscious focus.

Because the task at hand is so simple, and the soothing calm of the water reinforces the mundane nature of the task, it becomes easy to get lost in your thoughts while you are washing the dishes. Most people don't use this time as an opportunity, and instead obsess about the fact that they are upset about this chore. They may even feel that they've have been relegated to a life of mundane tasks and that their spouse is ungrateful for all they do around the house. The list of negative thoughts continues. No wonder most people hate washing dishes. With so many dominant negative thoughts during the task, who wouldn't avoid washing dishes like the plague? But, if you shift your mindset before you wash the dishes, you can look forward to the task as an opportunity to work on your goals and dreams.

Let's consider the following example to illustrate how to shift your mindset during a mundane task from a state of negativity to one of abundance and prosperity. Imagine if the latest celebrity spokesperson from Publisher's Clearing House knocked on your door and, surrounded by cameras and microphones, offered you a check for ten million dollars.[53] But, the gift of money comes with a catch. The celebrity spokesperson lets you know that for you to receive the check, you need to spend the next sixty minutes washing a pile of dirty dishes. That's right! The only thing separating you from having ten million dollars is an hour's worth of dishwashing duty. Seems pretty far-fetched. But, imagine your mindset while you complete the task.

How joyful would you be while you're washing those dishes? The word euphoric would even be an understatement. Why? Your ten-million-dollar dishwashing task is exactly the same as it has been every day for however many years you have been relegated to dishwashing duty. However, the thoughts you have of the reward that you will be receiving once the task is completed create a huge surge of dopamine in your brain. This surge is most likely so great that you would almost be floating on air while you scrub the grease off the pots and pans. Given this scenario, anyone reasonable would agree that the task itself is not related to your attitude about the task. The task is just a simple task, regardless of how you think about it. The functions of the brain that we have discussed throughout the book support that the thoughts going through your mind while completing a task are important, regardless of underlying task. Even while you are completing a task so mundane as washing dishes, if you can create a thought process that transforms you into a state as if you were about to win the lottery, then even dishwashing can become an incredible experience that you will look forward to.

You have to wash the dishes anyway, so you might as well use the time during your dishwashing experience to do what Napoleon Hill suggests in his book *Think and Grow Rich,* which is to visualize your success during the process.[54] When you think about who you want to become, Hill points out that your brain has no idea whether that thought is reality or imagination. Much like being excited at the prospects of getting a ten-million-dollar prize at the end or your dishwashing experience, you can be excited about the prospects of who you wish to become.

How do you do this consistently to make a lasting impact in your life? The answer is to use the time wisely and in a way that creates dopamine on two levels. One level is created because you want to take pride in finishing the task at hand and use it as an opportunity to check an item off your list. The second level is created because, as you take the time to visualize who you want to become, you become excited with anticipation. Because this task is simple, you can easily choose exactly what to daydream about. Remember, your thoughts are your choice and you can choose to create an amazing life with the proper focus.

As we have discussed, when you are excited for a vacation that you have already planned, much of the excitement comes from visualizing the future trip. As you get closer to your departure, you inevitably think about the plane flight, checking into the hotel, what you will be doing on your vacation and many more details. This is your reality because you know it's going to happen, so you get rushes of dopamine in anticipation of the planned trip. However, your brain has no idea that you are actually going on this trip. For example, if you wanted to go on the same type of trip, hadn't actually planned it yet, but spent the same amount of energy visualizing the trip and daydreaming about it then your brain would still release dopamine in anticipation of the trip. By daydreaming about a future that you are in the process of creating, you essentially fool your brain into a state of anticipation. If you consistently do this, as we disused in the chapter on visualization, you will move yourself towards this reality.

Additionally, you can choose to make a task like washing the dishes one of your streaks. Instead of simply writing down, "washing dishes" on your streak list, you can make it a little bit more creative for a greater impact. You can write down something like, "Spend 30 minutes daily visualizing my ultimate future self while cleaning my environment." Think about how much that will add to your life! You might even start looking forward to washing the dishes because, you're no longer just washing the dishes. Instead, you are actually entering into a meditative state that will allow you to connect with your sub-conscious and merge with the vision you have of your ultimate self. This meditative process and visualization will slowly reprogram your brain over time and allow you to start believing in this future self. This process will help drive you toward the vision you have for yourself. Additionally, because it's a streak, the further you get down the path of washing dishes, the more dopamine is released with the prospect of washing dishes. Understanding this dynamic will get you excited about many mundane tasks that are part of your routine because you will be creating a better future for yourself while you are doing them.

Now you understand why you can fall in love with a task that is as mundane as washing the dishes. Challenge yourself to be in the moment and to visualize your success while you are in the process of your daily mundane tasks. No matter how successful you are, you will have these types of tasks in your life. You might as well make the choice to use this time wisely.

*"A positive attitude may not solve all our problems
but that is the only option we have if we want
to get out of problems." - Subodh Gupta*

CHAPTER 22

No matter what, have a great attitude

Earl Nightingale is known by many as the Dean of motivational speaking and one of the first widely known, and widely syndicated success coaches. He said that about ninety-two percent of what happens around us, and to us, is completely out of our control. But we can always control our attitude, which is what shapes our life for better or for worse. I'm not sure exactly how Earl Nightingale came up with the number ninety-two percent, but what's important about his message is the focus on what you control. Logically, because you control your attitude and your attitude shapes your life, then you are thus responsible for how your life turns out. Think about "who" you are right now. Aren't you simply a representation of yourself in this particular moment? That is, you never really "are" someone, but are always on the path to "becoming" someone. This life is a journey that continues relentlessly, and we have no choice but to succumb to time. If we focus on always becoming someone better, then we can always be grateful for each moment because this moment is always the beginning of the next steps in our journey. Isn't the beginning where all the excitement is?

Too many people are victims of their past, victims of their negative thoughts, and victims of a limiting attitude. Admittedly, attitude is one of the hardest things to control because we have been conditioned to express ourselves based upon our feelings. It's as if our feelings are no more than a childish reaction to not getting what we want. Think about it. A bad attitude usually stems from some event in your current life that isn't producing the results you expect. The child within you then reacts and makes a choice to vocalize this event negatively to those around you and to yourself.

Your shift in attitude may stem from a situation as simple as someone taking the parking spot you were waiting for because a car that's backing out blocks you from the spot. You may feel that the person pulling into "your" spot is doing it deliberately because you know they saw you. You then might think to yourself, "How dare they take my spot!" Then, you sit there staring at them with a nasty look on your face, in hopes that somehow your laser like glare will convince them to apologize to you, get back into their car, and back out so that you can pull into the spot that was clearly yours. Then, because they are so distraught over their behavior, they will offer to purchase you lunch and to fill up your gas tank for you. But, alas, they get out of their car, completely ignore that you are there and begin walking to their destination without even giving you a thought. Now you think, "How dare they!"

Perhaps your parking lot rival saw you and perhaps they did not. They may have taken the spot purposely and they may have not. They even may have been ignoring you as they walked away. Or, maybe they didn't realize you were waiting for the spot they chose. In this moment, you have a choice. You can stew about what just happened, grip the steering wheel with white knuckles and storm off to find another spot. Worse yet, you can continue to obsess about the incident throughout your day. When you get to your office, you might dramatically tell your co-workers about this unthinkable offense that took place against you. As you describe the inequity of it, you get angry all over again and your description of the perpetrator paints them as a villainous wretch taking advantage of your patience and courtesy in the parking lot. You might even tell the story repeatedly throughout the day to others. Each time, you relive the event and hold on to it, verbally keeping it alive. Each time, you relive the negativity of your retold experience, as if it were still happening to you at that very moment.

Meanwhile, elsewhere, the offender who "stole" your parking spot is probably going about their business without a thought of the incident. They most likely had no clue about what they did, didn't take that spot on purpose and aren't living in the negativity of reliving the moment. But, even if they did do it on purpose, why would you let that action ruin your day? Every time you let someone else's actions affect your mood, you have just allowed that person to take your power. One of the most powerful actions you can take in life is to remember that you are writing your own story and can turn the page at any time. There is nothing saying that you need to revisit negativity in your life and complain about it as if when you don't get to express your story, you will somehow explode from the internal tension. In his revolutionary therapy method, Carl Rogers claimed that you are completely in control of how you react to stimulus in your life and the healthiest people are the ones who don't let external stimulus affect their internal value system and live a life in which their self-image is congruent with their actions.[55]

Rogers is not the only one who has made this assertion. As Don Miguel Ruiz explains in his book, *The Four Agreements*, we choose to believe things about ourselves and this can be good or bad, depending on the value we assign to our belief.[56] If you are walking down the street and someone yells out the window to you that you are ugly, then you are. But only because you made the choice to believe it. On the other hand, if someone whistles at you and says that you are beautiful (or handsome), then you are. But only because you made the choice to believe it. Being told that I was lucky after enduring a near-tragic accident of launching myself through a plate glass window when I was a small child made me believe that I was lucky. Even though I went on to face many more challenges in life, the thought of having luck on my side made me believe that I was destined for great things. Starting to be programmed like this at a very early age definitely helped me through many difficult times. Programming our brains to help guide us toward our goals is quite a daunting task, which is why many people fail at it and end up falling short of living their best life.

Self-programming is so important because, regardless of what happens to you, you need to have a basic belief about yourself that allows you to transcend any circumstance. Additionally, you can further help your own cause if you choose to address the challenges in your life with a positive attitude, regardless of your current situation or circumstance. Many people have been taught that life is a series of ups and downs, and how you handle the downs predicts the outcome. What if this belief about life is incorrect? What if your life really isn't a series of ups and downs? As Rick Warren described in his best-selling book, *The Purpose Driven Life*, your life feels a lot more like you are running on parallel tracks, with one track smooth as silk and the other rough as rocks.[57] That is, no matter what your circumstances, there will be wonderful aspects in your life but, at the same time, you will face some challenges. Maintaining a positive attitude becomes one of the most powerful actions you can take because it allows the important aspects of your life to move forward continuously no matter what else you are facing. The luck that I chose to believe in followed me around and helped me to maintain a positive attitude consistently because it stemmed from a powerful close call with death. Even through the toughest times, the scar on my wrist was always with me as a constant reminder that I am here for a reason. Although there were many circumstances that could have broken my spirit, my attitude and feeling of luck allowed me to persevere.

You probably have different challenges in your life from mine, or perhaps some are the same. Some challenges may be easier and some harder. Some may have overwhelmed you or may be currently overwhelming you. To reiterate: My goal isn't to retell the hardships I've had in my life and how I overcame them to inspire you. My goal is to share the secret of streaking so that you can program your brain to get past your own hurdles. My aim is also to share some best practices that will allow you to navigate this life and that will give you the best chance of an amazing outcome. Having a great attitude is a skill I highly recommend because it is an investment in yourself that will continue to pay you dividends throughout your life's journey.

"True mastery transcends any particular art. It stems from mastery of oneself--the ability, developed through self-discipline, to be calm, fully aware, and completely in tune with oneself and the surroundings. Then, and only then, can a person know himself." - Bruce Lee

CHAPTER 23

Learn the process of mastery

Daniel Kahneman is the Nobel Prize winning behaviorial economist that I referenced in my 2016 TEDx talk. He completely changed our understanding regarding how we think and became famous for discovering that the brain has two different systems, which are both used differently when we make decisions. For simplicity, Kahneman named them System 1 and System 2.[58] System 1 is the system we use to make most of our decisions. This system makes decisions quickly and without much thought. It can be thought of as the intuitive system. System 2 is the analytical system that we use for more complex decisions, taking its time to make decisions logically. In general, we use System 2 much less than we use System 1 because our brains want to use the least amount of energy possible. The importance of Kahneman's research is his finding that we use System 1 much more often than we should be using it, and we also tend to use it mistakenly when we really should be using System 2. This is one of the reasons that we often make bad decisions.

Kahneman found that System 1 is often incorrect in its decision making because it doesn't use much logic or analysis and just comes up with the answer that seems right. I think of it as the intuitive part of the brain that is wired to jump to conclusions and accept answers as correct without much thought. So that you can really experience how System 1 works for yourself, I've compiled a group of questions that Kahneman used in his research and will present them to you in order from the easiest to the most difficult. If you really want to understand how System 1 works, you should follow along with each example and then answer each question as quickly as you can. The quickness of your response is critical. You need to go with the first answer that pops into your mind because it will ensure that you are using System 1 to come up with your answer.

Just in case you are one of those people who wants to be the exception to the rule and needs to convince themselves of their own intelligence…don't. First, know that this exercise has been given to rooms full of Stanford, Harvard and Yale graduate students who mostly don't answer the questions correctly. Therefore, no matter your level of intelligence, it's irrelevant if you don't answer the questions correctly. Especially as they get more difficult. Second, it's important that you don't skip ahead to the answer so that you can actually learn how your brain functions because understanding how the two systems work is the path which you have to travel to learn how to achieve mastery.

To help you ease into the process, we will start with a simple question that most people can actually answer correctly. This should make you feel better about yourself and boost your confidence level. Then we can move on to harder questions, which you will most likely get wrong. Again, most everyone gets the harder questions wrong if they let themselves answer them as quickly as possible without allowing System 2 to engage in the process. To make it easier to complete the challenge properly, think of getting a reward for having the quickest time and not for having the correct answer. At this moment, you should put down this book and grab a timer (for most of us this would be the clock app on our phone) and then come back.

Now that you are ready to go, please read the following question as quickly as possible and then answer it as quickly as possible. If you can answer it correctly in under a second, consider yourself a genius. Remember, they only get harder. So, if there is any chance of you achieving genius status, take advantage of it now.

Ready…go!

Question 1: A bat and ball cost $100 when they are purchased together. If the bat costs $90 more than the ball, how much does the ball cost?

Hopefully, you answered that question in less than a second and, if you did, it's most likely that your answer was $10. It's a simple question and doesn't take much thought to get correct. However, if you did answer $10, then you answered incorrectly. But, don't worry, there are no more questions left and it was actually a difficult question to answer quickly. I set this up deliberately because I wanted you to think the question was easy so that you would go with your instinct when you answered. Hopefully, you now have a firm understanding of how System 1 works and why it's not the right system to use when making certain decisions. Again, you were tricked into answering as quickly as possible. Please know that you can still feel good about your intelligence because almost no one gets the right answer to this question if they use System 1 and come up with the answer quickly. If you had enough time and could have engaged System 2, you probably would've answered the question correctly.

The ball actually costs $5. However, almost everyone answers $10 (even Stanford, Harvard and Yale graduate students answer the question incorrectly when they have to do it quickly) because System 1 wants to use straight arithmetic without the help of logic. System 1 basically fools you into using the caveman part of your brain to think in large chunks. Basically, you subtract $90 from $100 to get the answer $10 because $90 and $100 were the only numbers you were given, and the answer you compute seems correct. However, the most important part of the question was noticing that the bat costs $90 MORE than the ball. This turns into a problem that needs several steps to come up with the right answer.

You can use an algebraic formula to calculate the correct answer. If you assign "y" to the value of the bat, and "x" to the value of the ball, then $100 = x + y (the bat and the ball combined are $100) AND y = 90 + x (the bat is $90 more than the ball). Next, if you substitute "90 + x" for the value of the bat, you will then need to solve for "x" using the formula $100 = x +(90 + x):

$100 = x + ($90 + x)

$100 = 2x + $90

$10 = 2x

$5 = x

Now, simply check the work. If the bat is $95 and the ball is $5, then it satisfies the solution. The bat is $90 more than the ball ($95 - $5 = $90) AND the total of the bat and ball together is $100 ($95 + $5 = $100). There is no way that your System 1 thinking process could have come up with this unless you are a mathematician and have spent years working on advanced mathematical concepts and proofs. This is a very important concept to understand because, if you want to answer these types of questions requiring System 2 by only using System 1, you actually can learn how to do it through extensive practice. This is a very time-consuming process but can be accomplished with streaking. Here is another key reason why streaking is such an important part of creating success in your life. Although the execution can be difficult, the theory and mechanics are rather simple.

In chapter seven, we discussed that creating belief in yourself can only occur once you've done something challenging that rewires your brain so that your synapses fire in a pattern of self-belief and confidence. Once your brain is rewired, you can call upon that pattern at will when you face other challenging tasks. However, there are two holes in this theory that streaking can be used to fill. The first hole is that the rewiring of your brain is usually very skill-specific and not applicable across all endeavors. This is why many professional athletes can operate at the highest level of their sport and make millions of dollars for their efforts yet end up going bankrupt five years after they retire. Although they have an extreme level of skill and confidence in their profession, which stems from their synapses firing at lighting speed to allow automatic performance at peak levels in their sport, they have not taken the time to transform that level of skill into other facets of their lives. The other hole is that sometimes your self-confidence can lead to over-confidence in an area where you are not skilled. This can lead to a false sense of security, which often leads to failure. It's the, "they never fail at anything, so they won't fail at this" fallacy.

Luckily, much like the 500-curl challenge that I conquered when I was twelve, people sometimes experience a life event that rewires their brain for global success. Because the event doesn't relate to a specific skill, it's impact can be felt more generally. No one is going to pay me any money to do hundreds of curls in a row because there's no market for it. However, because that life event gave me the confidence in myself that I needed, it allowed me to challenge myself with other tasks as I grew older. In that process, I developed some marketable skills. But, when someone has achieved excellence in very specific skill that has a short shelf life, but doesn't commit to learn another needed skill, it could be detrimental.

This is a common reality with athletes because their brains have become wired to succeed in one specific sport. However, many of them can't transfer that success to other professions, or even to sticking to a simple budget, because they are not globally wired for success. That is, they can't apply their skill set to other endeavors. In order to achieve success outside of a specific gift or talent, one must force other parts of the brain to fire. Luckily, the brain can accept as much skill development as you have time to commit. Therefore, the quest for mastery simply requires repetition, sometimes years of it. Once there are enough repetitions, the "thinking" part of the brain that requires analytics, logic and time to execute a certain task that starts out as very complex becomes faster and faster at executing that task. Eventually, System 2 is no longer needed and, for the sake of efficiency, System 1 takes over.

People who can do something very complex with speed and ease are thinking like this. They have taken the arduous time to shift System 2 tasks over to System 1 and they are operating subconsciously, which is what defines mastery. The problem is that most people stick with using System 1, make bad decisions because they should have been using System 2 and then form bad habits that are very difficult to break. They remain stuck in System 1 without any mastery, which leads to a life of mediocrity. The trick is to get there and back again while gaining mastery along the way. That is why the commitment to the long journey is so important. If someone just hands you the keys to the castle and you don't know how to rule the kingdom, your new-found station in life won't last. In his fable, *The Alchemist*, Paulo Coelho tells a wonderful story that illustrates this insight.[59] It's the story of a boy who sets out to find his treasure, is met with a long journey that is fraught with many challenges and eventually learns that his treasure was to be found in the very spot that he began his journey. However, the boy wasn't upset at everything that he had to endure to get right back to where he started because there is no way that he would have appreciated his treasure, nor would he have known what to do with it, had he not taken the exact steps that he did to find it.

You are where you are in life because of everything you have done up to this moment. You are reading the words in this book right now because of a series of circumstances that brought it into your life. You are in a relationship, out of a relationship, or wanting or not wanting a relationship because of every previous event that has occurred along your long and winding road. If you are thrilled with where you are, congratulations. If you aren't, congratulations as well because your best life is still ahead of you. There are always two questions to ask yourself at any point in your life: Do you know how to unlock the patterns in your brain that can lead you to the success you seek, and do you know when to quit if the vehicle you are using is not correct for you? These are both critical questions to answer because, as I've described, if you work hard at something that you will never excel at, then you will underperform and will never reach a level of mastery. To take advantage of this knowledge and understand how you can apply it to mastery, you simply need to understand how you can use the method described in this book to train System 1 to make the unconscious decisions you need to make quickly and correctly when you are facing System 2 challenges. When you can do this, you will make things that are hard look easy. When you can do this, you become a master.

If after many attempts, you can never get to the level where System 1 is being used to solve System 2 challenges, then you may be on the wrong track. It's not that you couldn't continue using your micro-goals to train your brain to work at maximum efficiency in your chosen endeavor, but you might never be a master. You can still live a very fulfilling and successful life whether or not you achieve mastery. But you may not ever work at your true calling. You may remain as the back-up singer that never becomes the headliner, the player coming off the bench that never becomes a starter or the golfer that never wins a tournament but makes enough money to stay on the PGA Tour. None of these examples are ones of failure. In fact, there are many people who never achieve true mastery in their given profession of choice and live very happy lives. Just keep in mind that if you apply the methods of becoming addicted to success to something that you can ultimately be the best at, then you will become one of the rare people who have mastered their craft and, as a result, will reap the rewards that come with that accomplishment.

"Today is the greatest day I've ever known." - Billy Corgan

CHAPTER 24

Perseverance

When my wife reads this, she won't be pleased…at first. However, like you, once she understands what I am conveying, I hope she will be. Matthew 6:34 is a verse in the Bible that I've always liked: "Therefore do not worry about tomorrow, for tomorrow will worry about itself. Each day has enough trouble of its own." No matter how hard the day is, no matter the obstacles in our paths, we can muster up the strength to make it through this day, which we call today. When you have finally found your purpose, are committed to something that you know is keeping you on the right path and things get so hard that you want to quit, go ahead and give yourself the permission to quit. But, don't do it today. Instead, make an agreement with yourself that you will quit tomorrow. That's right. Get through whatever you need to get through today and then quit tomorrow. The greatest thing about this method of quitting is that tomorrow never comes because each day you wake up, it's today again.

Please don't dismiss the power of this little trick. If you get into the habit of procrastinating on anything, always save quitting on something that's worth holding onto until tomorrow. Now, back to my wife's probable displeasure. Whenever my wife and I get into a knockdown drag-out argument and I can't stand the sight of her (and most likely, she can't stand the sight of me) I tell myself, "Okay, I will get divorced tomorrow." That may sound awful to you. But, know that I never say it to my wife and it's just an internal conversation. I do it because, after getting some sleep, the next morning comes and all the pain from the previous day is gone. More importantly, it's now today. I can't call it quits with her today because I can make it through any challenge or obstacle today, this one special day. You can apply this principle to anything in life because, since it's always today, tomorrow never comes. You can even use micro-goals if you need to and start a streak based upon your commitment to today. After all, you can do anything for a day.

You can get through the most difficult times in your life if you learn how to play little tricks with your brain to release dopamine and cancel out negative thoughts. You even can apply this theory to your goal of working hard. Dr. Bill Dorfman runs an amazing program that is held at UCLA every summer called LEAP.[60] I've had the honor of being a mentor in the program for many years and have witnessed it make an impressive impact in the lives of the participants from all over the world, primarily high school and early college age kids. Most of the kids who come to the camp come on a scholarship. The LEAP organization helps raise money to pay for their travel and tuition because the participants would not afford it otherwise. The kids are so ecstatic to be participating because they are committed to learning how to be successful in life.

Throughout the week, the program consists of classes and activities led by skilled professionals, each in their particular area of expertise. The participants are taught how to network, how to stay positive, and how to make the right choices about their associations.

Additionally, celebrity speakers engage with participants in breakout sessions designed to motivate them to be their best by giving them very specific advice tailored to them and to their circumstances. LEAP is an inspiring program and is where I originally introduced the concept of streaking and micro-goals, as well as the concept of "today" that I just shared with you.

On the last day of the program, all the children gather in one of the practice basketball gyms at UCLA to spend time interviewing mentors who come from almost every professional field. From movie producers to attorneys and every occupation in between, the kids have the opportunity to sit down with a leader in a field they might be interested in pursuing. The sight of seemingly endless rows of tables and chairs that fill three side-by-side basketball courts is quite impressive. Picture a massive ballroom with desk-style tables filling the room, all lined up in horizontal rows stretching from end to end. About one-hundred-fifty tables are stretched out across the gym floor, each with one chair for the mentor on one side and chairs for the students on the opposite side. Each mentor is individually introduced by Dr. Dorfman to the entire crowd as they walk across a stage and then are directed to their designated table. Once all the mentors have taken their respective seats, the first round of interviews begins.

With a bit of organized chaos, all the kids run to the mentors of their choice and sit across the table from them in groups of four. Those four kids come prepared with questions and get to interview the mentor for thirty minutes. There are four of these sessions back-to-back, so each mentor gets interviewed for two hours and each participant has the opportunity to spend time with four different mentors. Although the students were different each year, the questions they asked of me were quite similar. Every year there was always one question that just about every group asked: "What's the most important thing you need to do to be successful?" Answering that question correctly is critical. My biggest challenge was to leave them with something that was meaningful, useful and that they could easily apply. Additionally, since they have spent a week learning about success and are speaking to three other mentors besides me, I wanted the answer to be something that no one else would teach them.

To answer the question, I found it was easiest to share a quick story. I would tell them about what I experienced when I first started in my line of work. During my early days in the financial industry, I quickly realized that it was going to require an extensive amount of consistent work, so I would strategically pick a day and put myself through a "Hell Day." This day consisted of getting into the office early, working as hard as possible and leaving late. It was the kind of day that, after you arrived back home in the evening, you looked back and were, not only exhausted, but proud because you had accomplished so much in that single day. It was a day that you would fall asleep from exhaustion even before your head hits the pillow. The advice I gave the kids regarding success was telling them to pick a day each week in whatever career they choose and work as hard as I had described. Inevitably, they would ask me which day I would choose as my hell day, and I would answer, "Today." After the laughter died down because they thought I was joking, I would explain to them that I was being very serious.

One thing they needed to understand is that you can only live one day at a time, so the memory of yesterday's hard work dies the moment you wake up. Of course, hard work is exhausting, but when you're done, it's over. Hard work is not like working out in the gym. In the gym, the harder you work, the more the lactic acid builds up in your muscles, which leads to more soreness over the next few days. Whereas, after a day of hard work, with a good night's sleep, you awake completely rejuvenated as if the previous day had never happened.

Each new day brings you a fresh start and you can string together as many days of hard work as you need to.

After my business was sold and I had to rebuild my new team from scratch, I worked as though every day was a hell day for five years straight. There were no days off, no vacation and no excuses. I was forty-three years old when I started and didn't let that get in my way. Whether you are in your twenties and just starting your career or in your forties and starting over, you never need to make excuses and just need to work hard each day in order to give yourself the chance for success. One of the greatest parts of my journey was that I had spent twenty years building the knowledge and experience that I needed to be successful. So, building my new business didn't take long because I was willing to work. Was I guaranteed the success I found because of all this hard work? No. However, I was guaranteed failure if I did nothing. Given the choice between risking failure even if you work hard and guaranteeing failure if you don't, the obvious choice in life is to risk working hard.

To give yourself the best chance at success, you need to work hard each day, you need to work at something in which you have a love or have a talent for, and you need to play the long game. You must delay gratification on the way to your goals, and you also need to focus on your goals with unrelenting purpose. If you can become the type of person who can execute all of these things on a consistent basis then you put yourself in the position to achieve your ultimate goals. You might wonder what the key is to setting yourself up for the best chance at success. As discussed continuously throughout this book, the key is to combine setting micro-goals with the concept of streaks to reprogram your brain for success. This will allow you to stick to your plans over time and give you the best chance of actually achieving success because, even if you fall short of your ultimate goals, you will have accomplished a significant amount along the way.

"People overestimate what they can do in one year, but underestimate what they can do in ten." - Bill Gates

CHAPTER 25

Does streaking work?

One of the most important concepts in martial arts is bridging the gap. It not only refers to bridging the gap between you and your opponent, but also to bridging the gap between your current level of skill and the skill you ultimately need to become a master. The martial arts paradox is that you never truly become a master because there is always more to learn, regardless of the skill level you obtain. Therefore, there really are no masters in martial arts, just practitioners who continuously seek mastery. In martial arts, as in life, you are constantly seeking to attain the unreachable and must be at peace with the concept that your only goal today is to be better than you were yesterday. You can never ask more of yourself than this.

For people unfamiliar with the belt system of martial arts, it encapsulates the idea of endlessly seeking this mastery. Traditionally, there were no colors for belts. Students who started practicing received a white belt and it would be the only belt they ever received. Since the belt was (and still is) considered a sacrosanct symbol of skill level, it was never to be washed. Over time a white belt became so dirty that it eventually turned black. The black belt grew to symbolize mastery because, for a white belt to turn black, it took decades of training. Therefore, to bridge the gap between white belt and black belt, all that was needed for a student to do was to show up consistently for decades.

Because progressing towards a black belt took so many years of sacrifice, most practitioners would get frustrated at their lack of progress. Because of this frustration, very few students who began studying martial arts ever achieved the rank of black belt and would quit along the way. This was one of the reasons that the colored belt system was instituted. The colored belt system rewards each student who continues to participate and who learns the techniques necessary to advance to a new level. Each new colored belt symbolizes a student's level of accomplishment. The belts continue to get darker in color as the student progresses toward black belt. However, even with the colored belt system, only a small pool of practitioners who start in their respective martial art ever reach the black belt level.

Many schools then added stripes that can be attained within each belt color. A contributing reason is that every three to four months a student is rewarded with a stripe that is affixed to the end of their belt, which demarcates clear progression. After they collect four or five stripes, they get rewarded with the next colored belt. In essence, stripes have now become a micro-goal and are short-term enough in occurrence that more students persevere to become black belts than in the past. This one addition to the belt system has done more to help students persist in their efforts and eventually achieve a rank of black belt than any other prior modifications to the belt system.

Is the road to achieving a black belt any easier or shorter today than it was in the past? No. It still takes the same amount of time and the same amount of effort. However, even the most traditional martial arts schools recognized that to keep students on the path, the multi-year gap between white and black belt must be mitigated by allowing the students to attain multiple rewards along the way. Some martial arts schools even have a system that allows a student to count the days it will take to attain the next stripe. This provides an even shorter micro-goal. This evolution of the belt system has changed the incentive-reward system in martial arts from long-term to short-term focus and effort. This change has allowed many practitioners who don't naturally have the ability to delay gratification to achieve higher ranks because of the shorter-term rewards they receive along the way.

The motivational industry is much like the martial arts schools of years past. Although motivational programs have a tremendous amount of information that has been carefully developed to help people achieve everything they want in life, most people never have a chance to capitalize on that information. Consistently, motivational programs state that you must first believe in yourself. Then, the programs are structured around pumping you up and giving you specific information to guide you on your path. Regardless of the content or presentation, these programs assume that you already believe in yourself and have what it takes to follow through with their advice. However, if you don't truly believe that you can follow through with the solutions to life that the programs propose, how can you expect that they will inspire you to magically make the shift from self-doubt into self-confidence? If you don't have the ability to delay gratification and work towards a long-term goal, how will you be able to get through all the obstacles you will undoubtedly face along the way?

In spite of all the high-spirited jargon pushing people to become their greatest selves, few people can actually make this happen. In spite of the well-meaning intentions of their designers, motivational programs continue to fail the vast majority of their subscribers because the programs lack the substantive step-by-step plan to teach people how to follow through.

Eric Thomas states that the reason a lion is different than a gazelle is because a lion is wired differently. Yet, he doesn't provide a formula for rewiring a gazelle into a lion. Instead, he says that to be a beast you need to do what beasts do. You must wake up at 3:00am every day and want to succeed as much as you want to breathe. I love that attitude, but it's easier said than done.

David Goggins says that a couple of the most important steps you can take towards success are to envision your goals clearly and get rid of all the excuses holding you back from working towards those goals, because if you don't, then nothing he says will be of any use to you. He is a no-nonsense, no-excuses person who willed himself to success in both the SEAL program and the Army Ranger program. He has an incredible will power that drove him to his success. Yet, he doesn't explain how to gain this strong will.

Les Brown said that making his first million dollars wasn't the hardest thing he ever did in life. Instead, the hardest thing he ever did in life was to believe that he could make a million dollars. Yet, he doesn't give you the formula for how to take this most important step of creating that belief.

These are some of the most respected names in the motivational industry, and their material is outstanding. From the teachers mentioned above, to Jim Rohn, to Anthony Robbins and to everyone in between, I can list dozens of other well-respected motivational teachers who communicate the same exact wisdom. Every motivational teacher that I have referenced throughout this book is convincing and their steps to success are unparalleled. All have a great formula for success, but they don't focus on the formula for how you push yourself to achieve that success. My hope is that you will now be equipped to take the most important step of your life and streak your way towards self-belief. Streaking will open the door so you can follow through with all the suggestions that these great motivational speakers and authors provide. So many great programs provide tools to transform your belief into success. I want you to take advantage of the ones that resonate with you.

Streaking is a method allowing you to conquer that first unattainable step of believing in yourself that has been so elusive for so many who struggle to reach their goals and dreams. Streaking allows you to build your self-confidence, maybe the most important trait that you need to develop. Just as if you start out to attain a black belt, the amount of work and dedication it will take to achieve your goals isn't going to change when you use the streaking method. The road will still be long and hard. However, the micro-goals that you reach as you keep track of your streaks are like the stripes that you would gain along the way to achieve each colored belt. It's neither the goals nor the effort that changes. What changes is that you now have a tool that will bring long-term goal achievement into congruence with your short-term incentive-reward system. You will get rewarded with the dopamine you need to keep you sufficiently motivated to continue marching towards your goals.

If you are someone who doesn't truly believe in yourself, are insecure with your abilities, or you don't think that you can achieve your dreams then, congratulations, you are not alone. As was mentioned throughout this book, it's not your fault. You simply haven't been given the secret to tricking your short-term reward system into achieving long-term goals. Streaking is that secret. Inch by inch you can build your self-confidence, you can work toward your goals and you can keep your focus on shorter-term goals designed to help incentivize you toward your ultimate destination. You may not be wired for success yet. But, creating micro-goals and keeping track of the streak attached to each micro-goal will allow you to rewire your brain for success and give you the ability to follow through and move to your aim. There is no quick fix. This is not a six-week program that will be the cure for all your ills. Because every person is different, I can't predict or guarantee how long it will take for you to achieve self-confidence, to achieve your goals or to achieve your ultimate success. But I do know that you are now equipped to bridge the gap between where you currently are and where you ultimately want to be.

Good luck, God bless, and I extend my heartfelt best wishes to all those who take this chance of living their best life.

REFERENCES

1   Simmons, Michael. "The Way You Read Books Says A Lot About Your Intelligence, Here's Why." Medium, 10 Apr. 2020, medium.com/ accelerated-intelligence/the-way-you-read-books-says-a-lot-about-your-intelligence-find-out-why-c2127b00eb03.

2   Musashi, Miyamoto. The Book of Five Rings. 1St Edition, Bottom of the Hill Publishing, 2010.

3   Wikipedia contributors. "Karate Gi." Wikipedia, 24 July 2020, en.wikipedia.org/wiki/Karate_gi.

4   Weintraub, Jerry (Producer), & Avildsen, John G. (Director). (1984). The Karate Kid. United States: Columbia Pictures.

5   Taleb, Nassim Nicholas. Skin in the Game: Hidden Asymmetries in Daily Life. Reprint, Random House Trade Paperbacks, 2020.

6   "In Skiing, What Is a Black Diamond? (With Pictures)." WiseGEEK, 17 Aug. 2020, www.wisegeek.com/in-skiing-what-is-a-black-diamond. htm.

7   "Alchemy." Merriam-Webster.com. Merriam-Webster, 2011.

8   Roy et al., 2017, Distinct Neural Circuits for the Formation and Retrieval of Episodic Memories, Cell 170, 1000–1012 August 24, 2017 a 2017 Elsevier Inc. http://dx.doi.org/10.1016/j.cell.2017.07.013

9   Kahneman, Daniel. Thinking, Fast and Slow. New York: Farrar, Straus and Giroux, 2016.

10 Sinek, Simon. Start with Why- How Great Leaders Inspire Everyone to Take Action. London: Portfolio/Penguin, 2013.

11 Kahneman, Daniel. Thinking, Fast and Slow. New York: Farrar, Straus and Giroux, 2016.

12 McChrystal, Gen. Stanley, et al. Team of Teams: New Rules of Engagement for a Complex World. Illustrated, Portfolio, 2015.

13 Tamir, D. I., and J. P. Mitchell. "Disclosing Information about the Self Is Intrinsically Rewarding." Proceedings of the National Academy of Sciences, vol. 109, no. 21, 2012, pp. 8038–43.

14 Sherman, Lauren E., et al. "The Power of the Like in Adolescence." Psychological Science, vol. 27, no. 7, 2016, pp. 1027–35.

15 "dopamine." Psychology Today, www.psychologytoday.com/us/basics/dopamine. Accessed 22 Sept. 2019.

16 Berridge, Kent C., and Terry E. Robinson. "What Is the Role of Dopamine in Reward: Hedonic Impact, Reward Learning, or Incentive Salience?" Brain Research Reviews, vol. 28, no. 3, 1998, pp. 309–69.

17 Hofmann, Wilhelm, et al. "What People Desire, Feel Conflicted About, and Try to Resist in Everyday Life." Psychological Science, vol. 23, no. 6, 2012, pp. 582–88.

18 Ley, David J. "No, Dopamine Is Not Addictive: Please stop calling dopamine an addictive rewarding neurochemical." Psychology Today, 6 Jan. 2017, www.psychologytoday.com/us/blog/women-who-stray/201701/no-dopamine-is-not-addictive

19 Pavlov, Ivan Petrovich. The Work of the Digestive Glands / Lectures by Professor I.P. Pavlov ; Translated by W.H. Thompson. 2nd English edition, London : Charles Griffin & Company, 2020.

20 "Newton's Laws of Motion." Www.Nasa.Gov, www.grc.nasa.gov/www/k-12/airplane/newton.html. Accessed 10 Sept. 2020.

21 Kotler, Steven. The Rise of Superman: Decoding the Science of Ultimate Human Performance. 1st ed., New Harvest, 2014.

22 Wikipedia contributors. "Fight-or-Flight Response." Wikipedia, 9 Sept. 2020, en.m.wikipedia.org/wiki/Fight-or-flight_response.

23 Mischel, Walter, et al. "Cognitive and Attentional Mechanisms in Delay of Gratification." Journal of Personality and Social Psychology, vol. 21, no. 2, 1972, pp. 204–18.

24 Bauer, Isabelle, and Carsten Wrosch. "Making Up for Lost Opportunities: The Protective Role of Downward Social Comparisons for Coping With Regrets Across Adulthood." Personality and Social Psychology Bulletin, vol. 37, no. 2, 2011, pp. 215–28.

25 Tate, Karl. "NASA's Mighty Saturn V Moon Rocket Explained (Infographic)." Space, 10 Nov. 2012, www.space.com/18422-apollo-saturn-v-moon-rocket-nasa-infographic.html.

26 Robbins, Mel. The 5 Second Rule: Transform Your Life, Work, and Confidence with Everyday Courage. Illustrated, Savio Republic, 2017.

27 Ziglar, Zig. See You at the Top. Revised & Enlarged, Pelican Publishing, 1982.

28 "Sisyphus." *Merriam-Webster.com*. Merriam-Webster, 2011.

29 Elkins, Kathleen. "Mark Cuban Started a Stamp Company as a Kid and the Profits Helped Him Pay for College." CNBC, 21 Oct. 2018, www.cnbc.com/2018/10/19/mark-cuban-started-a-company-as-a-kid-and-the-profits-paid-for-college.html.

30 Isaacson, Walter. Steve Jobs. New York, New York; Toronto, Ontario: Simon & Schuster, 2011.

31 Sinek, Simon. Start with Why- How Great Leaders Inspire Everyone to Take Action. London, United Kingdom: Portfolio/Penguin, 2013.

32 "Clearing Corporation." Investopedia, www.investopedia.com/

terms/c/clearingcorporation.asp. Accessed 10 Sept. 2020.

33 Journal, Wall Street. "SPX | S&P 500 Index Historical Prices - WSJ." Www.Wsj.Com, www.wsj.com/market-data/quotes/index/SPX/ historical-prices. Accessed 13 Mar. 2020.

34 "High-Water Mark." Investopedia, www.investopedia.com/terms/h/ highwatermark.asp. Accessed 11 July 2020.

35 Kersey, Cynthia. Unstoppable. Naperville, Illinois: Sourcebooks, Inc., 1998.

36 Wikipedia contributors. "Gary Vaynerchuk." Wikipedia, 20 Aug. 2020, en.wikipedia.org/wiki/Gary_Vaynerchuk.

37 Lee, Bruce. Tao of Jeet Kune Do. Santa Clarita, California: Ohara Publications, Inc. 1975.

38 Gladwell, Malcolm. Outliers: The Story of Success. New York, New York: Back Bay Books, 2011.

39 Wikipedia contributors. "Circadian Rhythm." Wikipedia, 6 Sept. 2020, en.wikipedia.org/wiki/Circadian_rhythm.

40 Johnson, Marie. "4 Habits of Today's Most Successful CEOs." Ladders | Business News & Career Advice, 13 Aug. 2019, www.theladders.com/ career-advice/4-habits-of-todays-most-successful-ceos.

41 Maier, S.F., Seligman, R.L., Solomon, R.L. (1969). Pavlovian fear conditioning and learned helplessness: Effects on escape and avoidance behavior of (a) the CS-US contingency and (b) the independence of US and voluntary responding. In B.A. Campbell & R.N. Church (Eds.),Punishment and Aversive Behavior New York: Appleton-Century-Crofts, pp. 299–342.

42 Suddendorf, Thomas. The Gap: The Science of What Separates Us from Other Animals. New York, New York: Basic Books, 2013.

43 "brain." *Merriam-Webster.com*. Merriam-Webster, 2011.

44 North, Vanda, and Richard Israel. Mind Chi: Re-Wire Your Brain in 8 Minutes a Day - Strategies for Success in Business and Life. 1st ed., Capstone, 2010.

45 "The Decision to Go to the Moon: President John F. Kennedy's May 25, 1961 Speech before Congress." Nasa.Gov, history.nasa.gov/moondec. html. Accessed 10 Sept. 2020.

46 Byrne, Rhonda. The Secret. 10th Anniversary, Atria Books/Beyond Words, 2006.

47 Hill, Napoleon. Think and Grow Rich: The Original Classic. 1st ed., Capstone, 2010.

48 Jennifer Carroll. "Lessons from Jim Carey on the Power of Visualization." YouTube, 9 Sept. 2013, m.youtube.com/ watch?v=8RuAZSWt7e4.

49 Slater, Georgia. "Jim Carrey Reveals His Mom Was 'Addicted to Pain Medication' During His Childhood." PEOPLE.Com, 15 Aug. 2018, people.com/movies/jim-carrey-mom-addicted-to-pain-mediation-during-his-childhood.

50 Wikipedia contributors. "In Living Color." Wikipedia, 25 Aug. 2020, en.wikipedia.org/wiki/In_Living_Color.

51 Goggins, David, Can't Hurt Me: Master Your Mind and Defy the Odds. Lioncrest Publishing, 2018.

52 Masaru, Emoto. The Hidden Messages in Water. United States: Beyond Words Publishing, 2004.

53 Wikipedia contributors. "Publishers Clearing House." Wikipedia, 17 Aug. 2020, en.wikipedia.org/wiki/Publishers_Clearing_House.

54 Hill, Napoleon. Think and Grow Rich: The Original Classic. 1st ed., Capstone, 2010.

55 Rogers, C. (1959). A theory of therapy, personality and interpersonal

relationships as developed in the client-centered framework. In (ed.) S. Koch, Psychology: A study of a science. Vol. 3: Formulations of the person and the social context. New York: McGraw Hill.

56 Ruiz, Miguel. The Four Agreements: A Practical Guide to Personal Freedom. San Rafael, California: Amber-Allen Publishing, 1997.

57 Warren, Rick. The Purpose-Driven Life: What on Earth Am I Here For? Grand Rapids, Michigan: Zondervan, 2002.

58 Kahneman, Daniel. Thinking, Fast And Slow. New York, New York: Farrar, Straus and Giroux, 2011.

59 Coelho, Paulo. The Alchemist. San Francisco, California: Harper San Francisco, 1998.

60 "LEAP Foundation - Leadership Development Program & Resources." LEAP Foundation, 16 Jan. 2020, www.leapfoundation.com.

Andre Julian spent many years as a financial commentator on television networks including CNBC, Fox Business, and Bloomberg. Although no longer a commentator, he continues his work in the wealth management industry; has been a TEDx speaker, in addition to his other speaking engagements; holds both a master's degree and a bachelor's degree from the University of California at Irvine; holds the Certified Investment Management Analyst® designation administered by the Investments and Wealth Institute® taught in conjunction with the Yale School of Management; and holds black belts in several martial arts. Andre lives in Southern California with his wife, daughter and the family's two cats.